national museum
of singapore guide

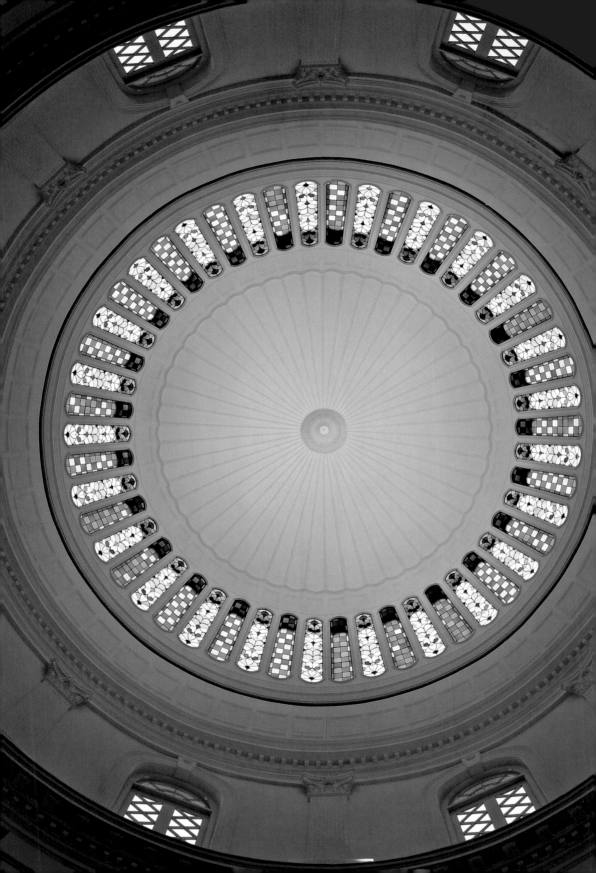

national museum of singapore guide

text Iola Lenzi
photography Jörg Sundermann

N M
S
**National Museum
of Singapore**

Editions Didier Millet

(Page 2) Ceiling of the original dome showing the now-restored stained glass windows.

(Right) View of the National Museum of Singapore from above showing the original 19th-century dome crowning the new Glass Passage that connects the old and new parts of the building.

(Page 6) A bicycle wheel from a display of vintage bicycles similar to the type used by Japanese troops during their land-invasion of Malaya and Singapore in 1941–1942. The bicycle-powered attack was as swift as it was stealthy.

Executive Editor
Melisa Teo

Project Managers
Hairani Hassan
Joanna Greenfield

Assistant Editor
Michelle Low

Contributors
Angelita Teo
Chung May Khuen
Sim Wan Hui
Tamilselvi Siva
Jason Toh
Wong Hong Suen
Cheryl-Ann Low
Iskander Mydin
Joseph Lim

Designer
Lisa Damayanti

Production Manager
Sin Kam Cheong

First published in 2007 by
Editions Didier Millet Pte Ltd
121 Telok Ayer Street, #03-01
Singapore 068590
www.edmbooks.com

and

National Museum of Singapore
93 Stamford Road
Singapore 178897
www.nationalmuseum.sg

Printed in Singapore.

ISBN: 978-981-4217-47-7

contents

(Below) The museum's time capsule located on the front lawn, commemorating 25 years of nation-building.

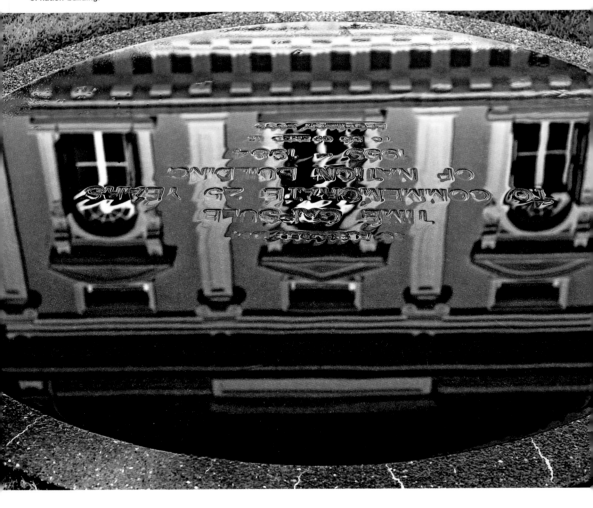

introduction

began my museum career as an assistant curator in this very museum in 1985. It was then a quiet and charming institution with a small running budget and partial air-conditioning, but rife with ghost stories. Apart from the public galleries, what happened behind the scenes had remained unchanged for decades. The corridor along the offices of the curators and the director was lit by a single 60-watt bulb, and cluttered with two huge cabinets of textiles and two drawers of our weapon and *keris* collection. All the assistant curators and museum assistants shared the spectacular space of the reference library, whose main features were its overwhelming height and narrow overhanging mezzanine ramp accessed by a steel staircase. Here we shared initially one telephone, two typewriters, and three walls lined with floor-to-ceiling bookshelves. Surrounded by the collections, books and the old handwritten notes of past curators and directors, I learned a great deal about Asian art in those few years under the watchful tutelage of the curators, Constance Sheares and Mrs Eng Seok Chee. It was indeed a very good time of discovery for a young curator.

Years later when I returned to embark on the museum's monumental redevelopment project, I would often be visited by this sense of discovery, or rather, rediscovery. By 2003, the National Museum had been overshadowed by the new successes of the Singapore Art Museum and the Asian Civilisations Museum. Although several waves of minor renovation had taken place, its old charm had turned stale. This long overdue redevelopment allowed us to take a step back to reflect on our past and plan for the unknown future.

We closed the Stamford Road building and moved to a defunct cinema in a shopping centre situated in the old warehouse stretch of the Singapore River. As if struck by amnesia, visitors forgot about the museum and gradually stopped coming. It was in this solitude that the new era of the National Museum was mapped out, our curators ploughing into the depths of the city's history (along with our own of 115 years), and our programmers seeking alternative ways to reach out to the public, through short films, tango dancers, and even a Barbie Doll dress-up competition. It was an exhilarating period of experimentation and discoveries about ourselves and our new audiences.

Spanning nearly four years from the drawing board to the installation of exhibits, the redevelopment has been a complex process, fraught with human and technical challenges. Yet, for all of us who were involved—the curators, project managers, foremen, architects, sound designers, engineers, exhibition designers, fundraisers, building contractors, programmers, lighting technicians, hospitality providers, and many more—the entire experience has been nothing short of enriching, indelible and rewarding. On behalf of this fantastic and energetic team, I am very proud to present to all our friends, old and new, the new National Museum, the oldest in Singapore.

Lee Chor Lin
Director
National Museum of Singapore

(Page 10) The museum's majestic north-facing façade where silver-painted shutters dialogue with the building's original Victorian architecture.

(Right) The museum's back entrance opposite Fort Canning Hill clad with specially-commissioned light-filtering mesh.

t

he National Museum of Singapore is the city-state's oldest museum. Though it has gone through a number of physical and directional metamorphoses over its 120-year history, the institution, remarkably, has functioned as a public museum without any significant break through the Sepoy Mutiny of 1915, two world wars, the Japanese Occupation, and the race riots that engulfed Singapore and the Malay Peninsula during the 1960s.

While the kernel of the museum we know today was sown in 1823 by Sir Stamford Raffles as the Raffles Institution, it was not until 1887 that the Raffles Library and Museum was finally opened in its own purpose-built Stamford Road building by the English Governor of the Straits Settlements, Sir Frederick Weld. Assembling anthropological as well as natural history material, some of which had been collected as far back as the early 19th century when the institution had first been mooted, possibly by Raffles himself, the museum's vocation in 1887 was to be a repository for artefacts deemed relevant to the flora, fauna and peoples of the region.

Housed in a domed and pillared neo-Palladian structure typical of the period's colonial institutional architecture, the museum was designed by English engineer Henry McCallum and erected by two successive teams of local builders at the foot of Fort Canning. At the time, some felt that Fort Canning Hill, as the building's backdrop, might compete detrimentally with the new museum and thus rob the institution of some of its grandeur. However, a century or so later, when plans were being drawn up for the museum's most dramatic and final expansion, its fortuitous positioning on the edge of historic Fort Canning Hill would eventually seem to be an asset rather than a drawback.

HE WHALE SKELETON

all the museum's displays, the whale skeleton is probably its most iconic. Fondly remembered by older museum-goers, the numental skeleton has, like a myth, over time, entered the popular imagination to embed itself in the collective memory of er generations of Singaporeans though these would never have seen it. In the early 20th century when the Raffles Library and seum was one of the few indoor public entertainment spaces the city offered its residents, large throngs habitually gathered the museum's galleries on Sundays and public holidays. It is therefore no surprise that the whale skeleton, first displayed Chinese New Year's Day 1907, proved a sensational addition to the already impressive zoological holdings, remaining one the museum's star attractions until its return to Malaysia in the early 1970s.

June 1892, a baby Blue or Indian Fin whale had been marooned and left to die on the shore at Kampong Sa'Batu, south of lacca. Aware of the Raffles Museum's excellent zoological collection and scientific reputation, the then Resident Councillor Malacca D.F.F. Harvey presented it with the 13-metre-long *Balaenoptera indica* skeleton that same year.

ck of space prevented its exhibition but when the Raffles Museum was re-opened on 13 February 1907 after a three-ar expansion and re-organisation, the whale skeleton—which was suspended on ropes in the passageway joining the old seum building and its new addition—gained immediate iconic status, marking the museum's renewal and entry into the th century. The skeleton was the pride of the museum until the early 1970s when the institution, divesting itself of its zoological lection, transferred it to the National Museum of Malaysia in Kuala Lumpur. Since 2003, the whale skeleton has been used in Malaysia's Labuan Marine Museum, but thanks to multimedia artist Matthew Ngui, visitors to the National Museum Singapore can still catch a glimpse of this legend when it periodically appears on the video wall in the Concourse.

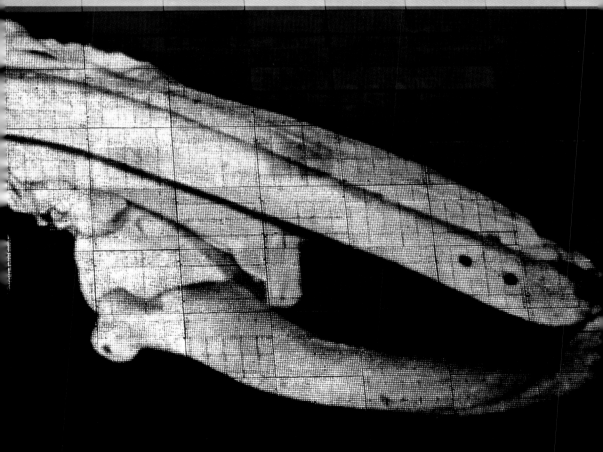

(Above) View of Suzann Victor's chandelier installation in action and beyond the Glass Passage.

(Opposite) Javanese-style figurine of a rider on a horse, recovered from the Empress Place archaeological site on th[e] banks of the Singapore River. This is, to date, the only one o[f] its kind found in Singapore.

At the dawn of the 20th century, Singapore, increasingly cosmopolitan, gained logistical importance. As the island's port and strategic geographic position as the West's maritime gateway to Asia generated growing international trade, the new museum's regional reputation and local popularity also grew. Expanding collections prompted the museum's extension in 1907, and by 1918, a specifically designated Singapore history collection had begun to be collated. In 1919, to celebrate the centenary of Raffles' Singapore landing, a fragment of the Singapore Stone that had once stood at the mouth of the Singapore River and had been in India since 1848, was returned to Singapore.

In the decades that followed, curators sought increasingly to document the social and cultural history of Singapore and wider Southeast Asia. Between the two world wars, the museum flourished as a centre for zoological, ethnological and anthropological research, forging bonds with similar institutions worldwide. The museum's

archaeological collections were also developed during th[e] period. And though the fall of Singapore in 1942 and t[he] subsequent Japanese Occupation heralded a slowing of wo[rk] at the museum, the institution managed to remain open [to] the public during these difficult years.

In the aftermath of the war, Britain gradually gave [up] her Asian colonies, with Singapore achieving independen[ce] in 1965. By then, the library, now known as the Natio[nal] Library, had seceded from the museum, moving to a buildi[ng] of its own nearby. This devolution gave the collections m[ore] space, and an art gallery was incorporated into the museu[m,] providing local artists with an exhibition venue.

In 1969, the museum became the National Museu[m,] and in 1972, as a key repository of the new nation's cultu[ral] heritage, took on an official nation-building role. Havi[ng] by then shed its Victorian identity as a vocationally-mix[ed] institution, the National Museum transferred its substant[ial] natural history collection to the National Museum alaysia and the then University of Singapore. The museum we know it today was beginning to take shape, with the st History of Singapore Gallery initiated in the wake of e museum's 1984 refurbishment. By the mid 1980s, the d institution was already moulding itself as a space and llection devoted to documenting and elucidating the mplex and layered history of the island's hnically, culturally and religiously verse migrant peoples as they came gether to form independent Singapore.

The early 1990s heralded the profound ansformations that have culminated in day's National Museum of Singapore. At e beginning of the 1990s, when it had come clear that the growing national llection of local painting, archaeological ares, Chinese and Southeast Asian hnographic material, and historical cuments relating to Singapore's colonial st could no longer be accommodated in a single entity, ngapore's newly established National Heritage Board lit the holdings into three distinct bodies, creating three fferent museums based on the collections.

The national art collection, now given over to the odern art of Singapore and the region, was from early 96 housed in Bras Basah Road at the new Singapore Art useum. A national collection of artefacts and antiquities cumenting the three majority cultures of Singapore, ith roots in the Chinese, Malay and Indian worlds, was stalled in the Asian Civilisations Museum, initially based Armenian Street, and later moved to its current Singapore ver location at Empress Place. Finally, the collection of tworks, papers and objects providing material evidence Singapore's pre-modern, colonial and post-Independence st would be displayed in the Singapore History Museum the original Stamford Road locale.

For several years, this historic venue served the Singapore story Museum well. By the turn of the century, however, had become apparent that in order to continue narrating ngapore's history in a meaningful and appealing way, the useum would need to rethink both its physical display d conceptual framework. It was decided to renovate the ilding and construct a new extension, with the aim to oaden the museum's cultural role by providing facilities r engaging the community with theatre, music and film esentations. Thus, in 2003, the museum left Stamford Road r its temporary quarters in Clarke Quay's Riverside Point.

…documenting and elucidating the complex and layered history of the island's ethnically, culturally and religiously diverse migrant peoples…

In late 2006, the Singapore History Museum prepared for its final metamorphosis. Returning to the Stamford Road building that had once been home to the Raffles Library and Museum, the National Museum, and then the Singapore History Museum, the institution changed its name one last time, becoming the National Museum of Singapore.

Emerging from a S$132 million renovation and expansion, and boasting an impressive 18,375 square metres of floor space, the new museum seamlessly meshes Englishman Henry McCallum's original late-Victorian architecture with the steel and glass of its modernist, Singapore-designed 21st-century annexe. As one of the city's most aesthetically stunning and functionally successful renovated colonial structures, the Stamford Road landmark, now fronted and backed by sculpture gardens, has, in its architectural splendour, moved beyond its role as a museum to represent Singapore's harmonious juxtaposition of old and new, Western and Asian.

The refurbished institution, that over the years has repeatedly changed locale, content and designation, has finally taken on the mantle of a history museum with didactic and innovative ambitions. Forward-looking in its approach to the past, the National Museum of Singapore presents Singapore's history from multiple angles. Through a variety of display strategies—including interactive media, technology and the language of contemporary art—the museum engages the public in a multifaceted exploration of the innumerable, intertwined strands of history that have played a part in making Singapore and her dynamic and cosmopolitan people what they are today.

HOW THE MUSEUM REMAINED UNSCATHED DURING WORLD WAR II

By the first few years of the 20th century, the Raffles Museum had consolidated its position as one of Asia's leading research institutions for the study of regional ethnology and zoology. Under the directorship of the German-born Liverpool zoologist Dr R. Hanitsch from 1895 to 1919, the museum prospered despite operating on a shoestring early in his tenure and during World War I. Hanitsch was succeeded by English zoologists Captain John C. Moulton and then Cecil Boden Kloss, who ensured that by the 1930s the museum was well established on the international scientific circuit. Kloss was followed by ornithologist F.N. Chasen, a renowned specialist of Malayan birds and mammals.

There is little doubt that the Raffles Museum's reputation as a centre of learning helped garner it protection as Asia plunged into war. As Japanese troops cycled down the Malay Peninsula in December 1941, museum staff turned their thoughts to storing the collections and boarding the building in anticipation of Japanese bombs and British counter warfare. Their concerns were to prove ill-founded.

When the Japanese finally arrived, the battle for the island's control was short-lived. The Stamford Road building took some shell hits, but these affected the library rather than the museum. And though looting was widespread, both museum and library were spared. More significantly, the Japanese administrators proved respectful of the museum. On behalf of the Japanese Emperor, himself a biologist, the English-speaking Professor Tanakadate visited Singapore's scientific institutions and took a particular interest in the Raffles Library and Museum, as well as the Botanical Gardens and its herbarium. When the Japanese army requisitioned the museum, he quickly replaced the military orders with his own, and to ensure the museum's preservation, had himself named Director of the Museum and Gardens.

Though the library was closed because its Western books posed a potential ideological threat to the new Japanese order, the museum was re-opened in April 1942, not even two months after the start of the Occupation. Tanakadate co-opted three British scientists to help him run the museum and gardens, viewing them respectfully as 'scientific colleagues in distress', and ensuring they remained in their research posts and out of the internment camps for most of the Occupation. The Europeans, for their part, discreetly hid some of the institutions' more sensitive and valuable material, such as Stamford Raffles' letters and a golden Malayan kris.

In September 1942, Marquis Tokugawa, a learned man with a keen interest in Malay language and history, took over the helm, and over time, more distinguished Japanese scholars worked at the museum and gardens. If conditions were difficult at times for the English staff, they were as good as could be hoped for under the circumstances. The museum's prestige had ensured its survival by attracting scientists who would use the institution, not pillage it.

Despite fears that intense shelling would mark the British army's return at the end of the Occupation, no real fighting took place. The museum passed once more into British hands in August 1945, and soon re-opened to the public on 10 September 1945. The Raffles Museum had, unlike Singapore, survived the Second World War virtually unscathed.

Singapore's only purpose-built, pre-Independence museum is doubtless one of the city-state's most reworked and rethought colonial buildings.

(Above) View of the museum's
dome from the ground outside.

The Raffles Museum's collection of natural and anthropological material began to be formed as early as the 1820s, but a building constructed specifically to contain it was only agreed to in 1882. Colonial Engineer Henry McCallum was assigned the job, and drew up plans for a standard neoclassical portico-fronted two-storey building. Though the design was eventually scaled down to reduce costs, the building would nonetheless retain the elegant rotunda and grandiose north-facing façade still familiar to us today. The 27-metre dome, the highest point of the Bras Basah area for years, proved particularly challenging to the first team of local builders enlisted by McCallum, which was dismissed after failing to come to terms with the complex and decidedly foreign structure of this classical architectural feature. The second team of locals managed it, however, and the museum opened its doors to the public in 1887.

Though the Raffles Museum's deep, sheltering entran portico and air vents above its doors and windows ma practical concessions to Singapore's tropical climate with its alternating heat and heavy monsoon rains—tl overwhelming effect was of a conventional public buildi in late-Victorian neoclassical style. On the inside, t museum's classical bent was as obvious as it was on tl outside; the circular, two-storey entrance hall under tl rotunda comprised four niches along its perimeter, design to accommodate sculptures portraying patrons of the a and sciences. Through the museum's history, these nich were seldom used in this way and have now been knock through to better ventilate the hall.

Despite being erected on a relatively modest budg the edifice was nonetheless considered worthy of certa costly features, such as the rotunda's stained glass and fis

(Above) The museum's original
grand central staircase.

ale zinc tiles, most likely imported from England, and the tricate foliate-patterned internal and external plasterwork orning cornices, ceilings and window frames. The cast-on railings for the upper rotunda balustrade so closely semble those manufactured for London's Royal Albert Hall at they were most probably not only crafted by the same glish firm, but also inspired by the very same pattern.

The collection expanded so significantly in the museum's st two decades that by 1907, a new extension was added hind the original structure, doubling the museum's floor ace. The two parallel buildings were then joined at their ntre by a bridge that, modified in the most recent expansion 2006, remains one of the museum's most distinguished chitectural features today. At the same time, the internal rought-iron staircase that spirals up from the second floor the storage areas in the eaves was introduced.

In 1916, the Raffles Library and Museum was extended yet again, this time in the form of a new library extension tacked onto the building's west side, thus freeing up more floor space. As the collection kept on growing, 1926 heralded another new extension, which was symmetrically positioned on the original structure's east side to balance the previous addition. As with earlier extensions, this was designed and built in the late 19th-century vernacular of the original.

THE NEW EXTENSION

If over its long history the museum has repeatedly changed names, it has, more significantly, also changed focus. Having departed from its Victorian-era study of natural history and consciously embraced its post-Independence role as a central repository for the material evidence documenting Singapore's history and its migrant people's heritage, the

COMPLETING THE NEW MUSEUM IN RECORD TIME

In the course of the National Museum's three-year restoration and construction, many hundreds of workers toiled to finish the new building in record time.

As with most construction sites on the island, the men assigned the laborious task of piling, digging, welding and building came from neighbouring countries in Asia. Workers from China, Burma, Thailand, Bangladesh, India, and Sri Lanka predominated though other nationalities were represented as well.

In order for the project to proceed at the necessary pace, the construction site was operational nearly round the clock, and the men—known locally as 'foreign workers'—were split into two 10- or 11-hour shifts.

Though most of the team provided general construction skills, certain workers possessed specialist knowledge. These included the plaster carvers from Madras, India, brought in especially to create and renovate the intricate and labour-intensive decorative stuccowork that adorns the Victorian-era part of the museum.

The skill required to manufacture this sort of cornice decoration has all but died out in Singapore and Malaysia, but, Victorian buildings still being common in India, subcontinental craftsmen able to restore them are plentiful.

Fortunately, some skilled architectural specialists remain in Singapore: both the rotunda's stained glass and fish-scale zinc tiles, though imported when the building was erected at the end of the 19th century, were restored by local master-craftsmen.

(Left) The old façade forms the backdrop of the Concourse, linking the old with the new.

31

museum now serves multiple and complex needs. In deciding to dramatically increase its floor space, the institution used the opportunity of structural renewal to fundamentally rethink its presentation of history. Thus, beyond the pragmatic tackling of the lack of space, the expansion project also sought to address the museum's diverse range of priorities, to facilitate its use of contemporary art as a tool for exploring history, and finally, to articulate the very essence of Singapore's past by architecturally echoing the layering of events in time that defines history.

Completed at the end of 2006 after three years in the making, the National Museum's 11,715-square-metre extension was a collaboration between Singaporean firms CPG Consultants—formerly a government agency known as the Public Works Department and privatised in 2003—and W Architects. As knowledgeable and experienced heritage-building architects, CPG Consultants had helmed the transformation of the 19th-century colonial buildings now housing Singapore's Asian Civilisations Museum at Empress Place and the Singapore Art Museum. This time, it was entrusted with renovating the old Stamford Road landmark and integrating it into a new and much larger scheme that would comprise a minimalist annexe. A year into the project, after excavation and building had begun, Mok Wei Wei and his firm, W Architects, became involved with the museum's design, with Mok conceptually directing the project.

To achieve the seamless marriage of new and old, Mok, with a modernist eye, sized up the original building's structural and spatial essence. Then, rather than highlight the decorative devices inherent to its Victorian vernacular, with his extensive use of white and grey paint, he underlined the old museum's spaces and volumes rather than its surfaces. A further playful reference to modernism is articulated by the building's scores of window shutters, all painted a luminous, shimmering silver, the effect subtly elegant yet thoroughly 21st century against the whitewashed neoclassical façade.

THE CHANDELIERS

Entitled *Contours of A Rich Manoeuvre*, the striking eight-chandelier installation hanging from the Concourse ceiling over the Link Bridge in the new extension was conceived and installed by Sydney-based Singaporean artist Suzann Victor.

Though the internationally established artist has created a number of chandelier installations over the years—the most famous version being *Dusted by Rich Manoeuvre*, which was presented in 2001 at Singapore's inaugural participation in the Venice Biennale—this piece was designed specifically for the National Museum of Singapore's Stamford Road site and has been present since the institution's opening in late 2006.

As well as being aesthetically engaging, the chandeliers are kinetic, programmed by Victor to swing over the Bridge from a height of 5 metres above its floor. Aligned 1.5 metres apart in a row, the red glass chandeliers oscillate perpendicularly to the Link Bridge below from morning until night in a combination of nine different 10-minute sequences.

While technically sophisticated, as a composition the work remains formally simple, the artist here favouring the gliding, rhythmic movement of the light fixtures rather than the violent interaction and fractured glass that characterise several of her previously conceived chandelier installations. With this work, the artist creates a slightly surreal effect since, contrary to what one expects of a light fixture, these eight chandeliers do not operate in a utilitarian way but rather, as mobile, abstracted objects.

Physically connecting the building's old extension with the new, the installation conveys a quiet but potent sense of tension, its poetic visual fluidity artfully combined with a tangible feeling of menace suggested by the fixtures' never-ending motion. This subtle but most deliberately thought-out exchange between violence and beauty is responsible for the work's mesmerising and dramatic effect. Further, thanks to their decorative aesthetic, Victor's ornate six-branch chandeliers, dangling sensually with ropes of ruby glass, offer a sharp contrast to the Concourse's minimalist environment and so neatly underscore the new extension's clean, rational definition of space.

Beyond its visual appeal, however, *Contours of A Rich Manoeuvre* also points, albeit allusively, to a historical theme of significance in Singapore and Southeast Asia: colonialism. The chandelier, imported to our region by European colonists, is a recurrent motif in Suzann Victor's œuvre specifically due to its Western, bourgeois associations. The artist uses the chandelier as an easily-read prompt, its repeated appearance in her work recalling Singapore and Southeast Asia's colonial past, and with it a defining component of our history.

Contours of A Rich Manoeuvre is one of the new museum's key pieces, signalling the institution's innovative approach to the understanding and interpretation of the past. Pointing museum-goers in new, forward-thinking directions as they explore history and its meaning in today's context, a work such as this one shows that contemporary art can embody powerful, significant and historically relevant concepts in a single visual flash.

(Left) View of the Glass Passage and the galleries beyond from the Atrium.

(Opposite) Unobstructed view of the dome through the Glass Passage's glass ceiling.

One of the largest frameless and self-supporting glass structures in the world, the Glass Passage…is a feat of engineering, its aesthetic and utilitarian aspects perfectly integrated.

When viewing the museum from the outside, many familiar with the old Stamford Road landmark will now observe a two-part edifice, its latest addition unobtrusively positioned behind the original building's stately Victorian façade; from the inside, however, the space works as a fluid whole, its layered juxtaposition of old and new as exciting as it is rational. The museum's original grand central staircase, located behind the entrance hall's small but majestic rotunda, is now instrumental as the main means of access leading from the old building toward the new exhibition spaces and expansive volumes at the rear.

At the start, architects and engineers faced considerable difficulties, namely, civic district conservation constraints limiting the new extension's height to the base of the original structure's cupola, and the challenges posed by the museum's positioning at the foot of rocky Fort Canning Hill. Yet, interestingly, these obstacles were not only overcome, but also provided formal direction and stylistic impetus to the project. The height restrictions unequivocally determined that in order to gain substantial space, much of the museum's new annexe would have to be built underground. Thus, the cavernous and pillar-free exhibition areas are literally carved out of the side of Fort Canning Hill. In the end, the expensive excavation process that initially seemed to weigh the project down also inspired Mok's choice of design and materials.

The most significant challenge of Mok's design brief wa not so much the building of a stunning modernist extensio as it was the conception of the new, enlarged museum a a coherent and seamless whole. Thus, Mok gave as muc thought to optimising the flow of internal traffic from ol building to new annexe, and to devising the appropria architectural language for the small but key transition area that linked old and new sites, as to the actual form of th museum's glass and metal extension.

One such link, the Glass Passage connecting the secon storey of the old building to the Atrium, is a masterf work of both architectural and conceptual genius. One the largest frameless and self-supporting glass structure in the world, the Glass Passage, which took nearly a yea to complete, is a feat of engineering, its aesthetic an utilitarian aspects perfectly integrated. But beyond i technical prowess and formal elegance, the corridor provide an intellectual transition between the old and new: its gla substituted for the original building's pitch tiled roo the walkway opens onto the sky and frames the Victoria cupola—which is visible close-up for the first time in i history—camped squarely on its axis. Thus, through the u of architecture, an active exchange between the Victoria and the contemporary has been established, and histor vividly conceptualised in the very fabric of the building.

THE VIDEO WALL

Located in the middle section of the black concrete-clad partition that runs the length of the Concourse, is Singaporean multimedia artist Matthew Ngui's large-scale, silent video work *The Building Remembers/Remembering the Building* (2006). Ngui, one of Singapore's most internationally recognised conceptual artists, is known for his thematic focus on history and culture. With this interactive and changing video, he has produced a work that is not just about history but also actively documents and creates history.

Positioning an LED screen behind the concrete, and embedding hundreds of thousands of acrylic rods deep into the wall so that, perforating its surface, they let the image through from the screen behind, Ngui has, with technology, transformed passive architecture into a living work of art. But if its construction is technically sophisticated, its thematic content is straightforward.

To achieve his multi-prismatic effect, Ngui screens three different types of visual material that alternate randomly throughout the day. A first type of projection presents still black-and-white archival photographs relating to the museum, thus constructing a literal narrative of the institution over the last 120 years.

A second set of images is created by a camera capturing museum visitors in a designated space in the Glass Atrium; these portraits are then projected randomly on the video wall at a later time. Archived forever, this record of museum visitors constitutes a new and constantly expanding data bank of museum history. Thus, the museum's 'memory', by way of its camera-recorded patrons, is being formed, preserved and re-presented to the public, Ngui's video installation actively involved in the process of transforming present-day reality into history.

Another video camera, also located in the Atrium, creates the third set of images by capturing the movements of museum-goers as they explore the museum and transmitting this information back to the screen via 'live feed' (but without retaining any data), so the film's subjects may catch themselves on film as they roam around the Atrium.

The sequential unpredictability of the projection, with images never repeated in the same order, lends the work a permanent freshness that could not have been achieved with looped film. More importantly, Matthew Ngui's work shows how art can be made to convey complex ideas relating to time, history, and the multiple and differing perceptions of reality that combine to form 'truth'.

(Below) View of the museum's
rear entrance and the bronze
Pedas Pedas, one of the
institution's commissioned
outdoor sculptures.

(Page 42) Aerial view of the
museum looking southeast.

Another of the museum's outstanding design features is the black-tinted concrete flooring and wall cladding throughout its new extension. Again, the project's design team has sought to connect architectural vision with the functional and spatial demands of the building. Beyond the 6-metre gap separating new extension from old edifice— mandated by the Urban Redevelopment Authority—a massive, three-storey cantilevered wall that marks the new extension's formal appearance is backed to the rear by another wall dressed in these gigantic black slabs. Low-tech and hand-finished, these never-quite-the-same concrete tiles lend the new architecture a layered and sometimes rough, earthy appearance that recalls the very stone of Fort Canning Hill from which the new space was carved.

As well as referencing the actual stone present during the excavation process, the striated appearance of the concrete also alludes materially to the juxtaposition of the historic and contemporary structures incorporated into the enlarged museum. Finally, and perhaps even more allusively, the concrete slabs suggest the layering of Singapore's social fabric as waves of migrant peoples landed on the island's shores, moulding its history. Beyond creating visual drama and prompting visitors to consider new perspectives, the black wall running the length of the annexe's first floor supports local experimental art, incorporating into its very structure Singaporean multimedia artist Matthew Ngui's evocative LED video history of the museum.

If the concrete floor is marked by a somewhat industrial feel, then the entrance pavilion of the new extension, looking onto the green curtain of Fort Canning Park, can

At home against its natural backdrop, the rectangular construction…
is sufficiently raw and stark to eliminate any possible confusion with
Singapore's most ubiquitous architectural genre: the shopping mall.

be described as positively minimalist, only divulging what is housed inside with the huge lettering identifying the museum. At home against its natural backdrop, the rectangular construction—clad in champagne-coloured corrugated meshing—is sufficiently raw and stark to eliminate any possible confusion with Singapore's most ubiquitous architectural genre: the shopping mall.

Indeed, the museum-goer, progressing from back entrance to front, finds himself moving through zones of increasing refinement. Starting in nature (at Fort Canning Hill), which is regarded by most as the ultimate expression of the untouched, he proceeds to the formally pure rectangular box marking the building's back entrance, then to striated, black-tinted concrete walls and flooring, on to the glass and polished aluminium of the Glass Rotunda and Glass Passage, until finally ending up in the museum's chronological starting point: the highly aestheticised, surface-dominated Victorian building that has been gracing Stamford Road since 1887. The visitor sensitive to this thoughtful architectural progression will inevitably make the connection between the museum's framework and its content.

Housed since 2006 in a spectacular and awe-inspiring building that successfully marries the historical with the contemporary, the National Museum of Singapore has a plethora of tools at its disposal for the forward-looking presentation of history. Though its iconic building alone cannot be relied upon to fulfil the museum's challenging mission, it nonetheless plays a vital and significant role in presenting the optimal conditions for taking Singapore's and the region's past into the future.

IS THE MUSEUM HAUNTED?

Whether one believes in them or not, ghosts and their stories find a place in all cultures. Singapore, of course, has its own ghost stories, with one of its most intriguing set in what we know today as the National Museum of Singapore. This particular story involves the museum's last expatriate director before Singapore's independence, Dr Carl Gibson-Hill.

A Cambridge-educated medical scientist, Gibson-Hill, who had arrived in Singapore in December 1941 shortly before the surrender of the British, spent the Japanese Occupation interned at Changi. In 1947, he was appointed Curator of Zoology of the Raffles Museum and was subsequently made the museum's director. In August 1963, Gibson-Hill died unexpectedly only a few days before he was to leave his museum directorship.

The academic's death, the circumstances of which were shrouded in secret, sparked much interest and speculation in the press and population. Some, believing the director ill and weighed down by personal problems of an unknown nature, suggested he had committed suicide. While *The Straits Times* reported the cause of his death as an overdose of sleeping pills while bathing in his Seton Close home, other, non-official sources, proposed he had hanged himself in his museum office.

Those who believe that the ghosts of suicide victims chronically revisit the site of death will not be surprised to learn that since 1963, there have been numerous ghost sightings at the museum. Night watchmen in particular have confirmed the presence of a nocturnal visitor resembling Gibson-Hill in both appearance and manner, and some museum attendants today, though never having known Carl Gibson-Hill at all, are quite certain they have seen something, someone gliding through the darkened halls at night, ascending the old wrought-iron spiral staircase that connects the museum's second floor with the eaves above...

(Page 44) Looking up through the Glass Rotunda which houses the 360° screen.

(Left) Original museum corridor, now the Glass Passage, leading to the Living Galleries.

(Below) Spiral walkway leading to the History Gallery.

t he National Museum of Singapore, housed since late 2006 in a magnificently restored and expanded Victorian/modernist complex in the heart of the city's Civic District, boasts the longest and most distinguished cultural history in Singapore. Its vocation as a museum having changed repeatedly in the course of its long past, the institution only truly began to assume the mantle of a history museum in the early 1990s. Including the History Gallery—located at the base of the Glass Rotunda—and four Singapore Living Galleries that narrate history through the broadly accessible subjects of food, film, Chinese street opera, photography and fashion, the National Museum of Singapore uses art, technology and popular culture in innovative and engaging ways to present the complexities of the country's past and the layered, multicultural identity of its people.

Located on the second floor of the 19th-century part of the museum, on either side of the Rotunda, the Living Galleries cover a floor area of 1,321 square metres. They explore Singapore's past through its evolving popular culture, providing visitors with a narrative of the lives of both everyday folk and the social elite.

Examining food, fashion, film and Chinese street opera, with a particular focus on the nation-building years of the 1950s to the 1970s, and photography from pre-independent Singapore, the four galleries share a common interest in local culture's hybrid nature stemming from its often-mixed Chinese, Indian, Malay and European origins.

With close-up, extensive archival research, anecdotally-based study of the everyday, and their exploitation of the latest in filmmaking, graphic, lighting and design techniques, these Living Galleries impart to museum-goers much sociological and historical information in a non-academic but thought-provoking form.

...the National Museum of Singapore uses art, technology and popular culture in innovative and engaging ways to present the complexities of the country's past and the layered, multicultural identity of its people.

(Page 48) The 360° screen seen from inside the Glass Rotunda. Viewers can watch the film from either the Atrium level ramp or from the ground floor below.

(Below) Montage of images from *Singapore 360°*. This scene shows National Service recruits having their heads shaved in preparation for duty.

THE GLASS ROTUNDA

More than an interesting architectural feature of the museum's modernist 2006 annexe, the 15-metre-high Glass Rotunda plays a key role in introducing the History Gallery. Positioned at the eastern extremity of the upper floor's light-filled Atrium, the sometimes-transparent cylinder acts as the physical ingress to the History Gallery on the first floor below. Originally designed by CPG Consultants and GSM Design Inc. to respond conceptually and aesthetically to the Victorian wing's late 19th-century stained-glass cupola, the Glass Rotunda's basic structure was later inherited by architect Mok Wei Wei, who conceived the space as an innovative and changing motion picture screen.

Functioning differently according to the time of day, Mok's drum, through which the museum visitor spirals down to the gallery below on a smooth Guggenheim-style ramp, acts as a 360-degree cinema during daylight hours. In the course of his descent, the museum-goer is here shown a mosaic-like kaleidoscopic film depicting today's Singapore. Thus, by playfully introducing 700 years of Singapore history with scenes of the everyday, the museum succeeds, with this unusual but engaging presentation, in making sense of what might otherwise seem rather dry and possibly irrelevant. Once again, the museum's strategy of using technology and contemporary art in tandem serves to broaden history's appeal as well as widen its scope of relevance.

At night, the Glass Rotunda promises more surprises: transformed into a 24-metre-diameter translucent lantern, the structure lights up the city skyline with images projected not to those inside this time but onto its outer shell for all external passers-by to enjoy. This act of sorcery is achieved thanks to the superposition of several 'skins' forming the Glass Rotunda's surface. Behind the outside layer of glass are a perforated metal mesh as well as a blackout curtain and inner glass. According to how these are positioned, the projected film appears either on the inner side, with the blackout curtain lowered, or on the cylinder's outer surface, when the curtain is raised and the light from the projectors permitted to shine outward. The awe-inspiring Glass Rotunda, didactic during the day, takes on the role of a pure work of art at night, providing as it does a unique, technically sophisticated framework for new and innovative video and film creation.

(Below) Gold ornaments discovered in 1928 on Fort Canning Hill. The repousse-work plaque with flexible chains depicts the *kala*, a Hindu-Javanese protective symbol also known as *banaspati* and *kirthimukha*. The *kala* motif is a common feature of Javanese temples dating from the 8th to the 14th century. The two earrings on its left are set with diamonds, and each has a bar-and-socket joint and wire hinge.

(Right) A view of the Temasek Gallery, featuring 14th-century artefacts from Fort Canning Hill. The artefacts include gold ornaments, Chinese porcelain, earthenware, and glass items.

At the bottom of the Glass Rotunda's corkscrew ramp, the 2,800-square-metre History Gallery opens chronologically with the Temasek Zone, which explores Singapore's earliest documented pre-colonial history. Here, through archaeological material, including pottery shards found on the Singapore riverbed, the famously enigmatic Singapore Stone fragment, and the Javanese-style gold ornaments from the Majapahit period unearthed on Fort Canning Hill in 1928, the visitor is presented with tangible evidence of the island's early settlement.

A 10-minute film, *Sejarah Singapura: Picture of 14th Century Singapore*, directed by Ho Tzu Nyen proposes several hypotheses on the origins of Temasek's first inhabitants and rulers. Amongst the source documents quoted is the *Sejarah*

Melayu (Malay Annals). Combining historical fact and myth, the text was compiled and revised by the Malaccan court from the 16th century; though mentioning Singapura in several places, it was once considered tainted by its mythological content, and discounted as a relevant historical source. In recent years, however, with new information revealed by archaeological finds, the text has been re-evaluated and attributed greater credibility as a historical source. Two copies of the manuscript are exhibited here.

This comprehensive approach to the telling of history, where a lack of certainty is exposed, rather than hidden, underscores the museum's commitment to portraying Singapore's past candidly and from different perspectives, adopting the broadest possible viewpoint.

This comprehensive approach to the telling of history, where a lack of certainty is exposed, rather than hidden, underscores the museum's commitment to portraying Singapore's past candidly and from different perspectives, adopting the broadest possible viewpoint.

...taking the visitor into the very heart of unfolding events rather than affording him the limited view of a passive, sideline observer.

(Page 58) A scene from the film *Sejarah Singapura: Picture of 14th Century Singapore*.

(Left) In this pathway called 'Arrival', a mural landscape depicts the seaward approach to what would eventually become the Singapore entrepot.

(Right, above) The Singapore Stone—a fragment of inscribed sandstone from a larger monolith once sited at the mouth of the Singapore River—is the earliest written document found to date in Singapore. The original boulder revealed about 50 lines of either Sumatran or Javanese inscription, possibly dating from as far back as the 10th century.

(Right, below) The re-created courtyard of Thian Hock Keng temple sets the stage for the narration of the story of one of Singapore's earliest and most prominent traders and philanthropists Tan Tock Seng.

From here, as visitors move into Singapore's colonial era, they are free to choose between two different ways of approaching Singapore history: those keen on exploring its major headline events will do so via the **Events Path**, while those interested in the effects of the same history on the man on the street will elect the **Personal Path**. Though it is possible to follow one or the other path singly, it is also quite feasible to move from one to the other and back, this meandering between paths taking the visitor into the very heart of unfolding events rather than affording him the limited view of a passive, sideline observer.

(Left) A rare letter written by Sir Stamford Raffles in Singapore in January 1823 during his last visit to the island. The letter contains Raffles' description of a booming Singapore entrepot.

(Below) A portrait of Sir Stamford Raffles painted in 1817 by British artist George Francis Joseph. It was executed in the aftermath of Raffles' knighthood, conferred on him by the Prince Regent in recognition of his services in Java.

(Opposite) A display of several natural history drawings from the collection of William Farquhar, first British Resident of Singapore (1819–1823). The drawings were executed by Chinese artists in Malacca.

...cover every aspect of Singapore's transformation from commercial outpost to migrant colony to independent developed nation.

Eight distinct zones take the visitor from the landing of Sir Stamford Raffles in Singapore in 1819 and the island's subsequent colonial settlement by the British, right through World War II to self-government, union with and then separation from Malaysia, and finally, the trials and economic development of the post-Independence period. Entitled *Arriving, Settlement, Emporium, Port-city, Modern Times, Fortress and Syonan-to, Merdeka* and *New Nation*, these thematic sections cover every aspect of Singapore's transformation from commercial outpost to migrant colony to independent developed nation.

In quest of a balanced and open historical approach, events and personalities from the Chinese, Malay, Eurasian, European, Indian and Middle Eastern communities of Singapore, the museum's account often presents different and opposing viewpoints. For example, the conflicting British and Dutch claim over Singapore in the period following Raffles' landing is evoked in a lively audio presentation inspired by the actual letters sent during the wrangling by Raffles and the Dutch Governor-General of Java, Baron Godert Alexander van der Capellen to their respective governments in London and The Hague. This dramatised two-sided account of history not only brings events closer but also affords a clearer understanding of the unfolding situation's many complexities.

262

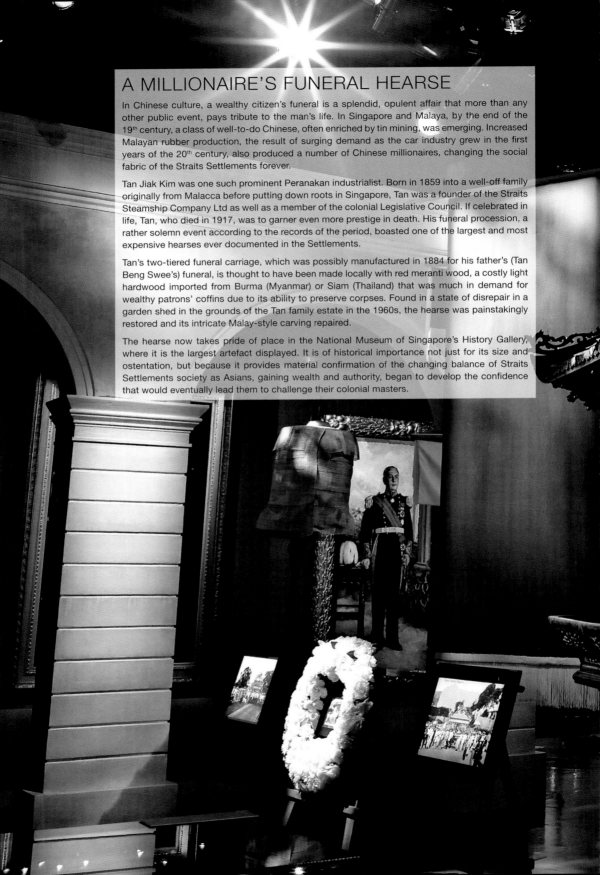

A MILLIONAIRE'S FUNERAL HEARSE

In Chinese culture, a wealthy citizen's funeral is a splendid, opulent affair that more than any other public event, pays tribute to the man's life. In Singapore and Malaya, by the end of the 19th century, a class of well-to-do Chinese, often enriched by tin mining, was emerging. Increased Malayan rubber production, the result of surging demand as the car industry grew in the first years of the 20th century, also produced a number of Chinese millionaires, changing the social fabric of the Straits Settlements forever.

Tan Jiak Kim was one such prominent Peranakan industrialist. Born in 1859 into a well-off family originally from Malacca before putting down roots in Singapore, Tan was a founder of the Straits Steamship Company Ltd as well as a member of the colonial Legislative Council. If celebrated in life, Tan, who died in 1917, was to garner even more prestige in death. His funeral procession, a rather solemn event according to the records of the period, boasted one of the largest and most expensive hearses ever documented in the Settlements.

Tan's two-tiered funeral carriage, which was possibly manufactured in 1884 for his father's (Tan Beng Swee's) funeral, is thought to have been made locally with red meranti wood, a costly light hardwood imported from Burma (Myanmar) or Siam (Thailand) that was much in demand for wealthy patrons' coffins due to its ability to preserve corpses. Found in a state of disrepair in a garden shed in the grounds of the Tan family estate in the 1960s, the hearse was painstakingly restored and its intricate Malay-style carving repaired.

The hearse now takes pride of place in the National Museum of Singapore's History Gallery, where it is the largest artefact displayed. It is of historical importance not just for its size and ostentation, but because it provides material confirmation of the changing balance of Straits Settlements society as Asians, gaining wealth and authority, began to develop the confidence that would eventually lead them to challenge their colonial masters.

(Below) Shortly after the British surrender, the Japanese army undertook the *Sook Ching* Operation, screening thousands of local Chinese and executing those suspected of anti-Japanese leanings. The stamp on the reverse of this photograph indicates that the girl had been cleared of any anti-Japanese activity. Behind is a televised clip of present-day Changi Beach where, in 1942, Chinese men were executed.

(Right, above) Pathway leading to the **Personal Path** component corresponding with the years of the Japanese Occupation (1942–1945). Here, the war years are represented as seen through the eyes of local teenagers.

(Right, below) This display case presents artefacts and documents relating to the late World War II heroine Elizabeth Choy and her experience of the Japanese Occupation.

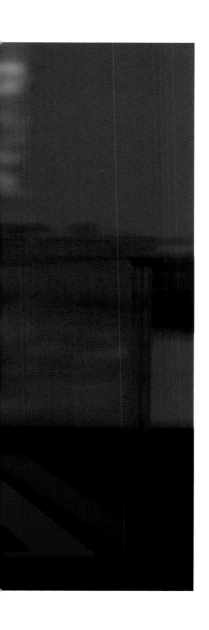

Further, curators, whenever possible and relevant, have sought to broaden historical investigation beyond Singapore's borders, providing information about the regional and sometimes international repercussions derived from incidents that were based in Singapore. For instance, the audio-guide presentation relating to the **Personal Path** in the World War II *Fortress and Syonan-to* zone features a short but enlightening interview with two local Indian women recruited as teenagers to serve in the Indian National Army (INA). The INA was formed during World War II by Indian nationalists and prisoners-of-war dedicated to winning India's independence from the British. The women speak about how they volunteered for the INA in Singapore during the Japanese Occupation, and were led on a march through Malaya, Thailand and Burma, with the goal to ultimately cross the border into India.

In addition, visitors wishing to further their knowledge of Singapore's relationship with the world at different points in history can, through their audio companion, access *Singapore and the World*, which features interviews with academics discussing specific topics relevant to themes addressed in each of the History Gallery's eight zones.

(Left) Old street signs displayed in the History Gallery.

(Below) A montage of advertising trays reflecting popular brands of the late 1940s and 1950s.

(Opposite) A video wall showing Singapore scenes from the 1950s. One screen shows people going about their lives; the other captures the buzz leading up to the 1955 and 1959 elections.

(Page 72) A scene from the video *August 9th*. The film is a montage of excerpts taken from the televised National Day Parades held annually since 1966.

...Singapore's complex modern history is portrayed from multiple and sometimes conflicting and anti-establishment viewpoints.

Comprehensive in its coverage, the museum does not retreat from thorny socio-political topics. Social worker Constance Goh, who, despite staunch church opposition and social conservatism, fought to introduce family planning to Singapore's women in the late 1940s, is heralded in the *Merdeka* zone. This space is also dedicated to the electoral politics of the 1950s which witnessed the arrival of new leaders such as David Marshall and Lim Yew Hock, both of whom eventually became Chief Ministers of Singapore. Their foray into local politics is documented through radio broadcasts, television footage and interviews. The creation of Barisan Sosialis, the main opposition to the still-in-power People's Action Party during the 1960s, and the role played by Lim Chin Siong in the Barisan Sosialis, is also discussed in the *New Nation* section.

Nuance rather than mono-track orthodoxy is manifest throughout the History Gallery, where Singapore's complex modern history is portrayed from multiple and sometimes conflicting and anti-establishment viewpoints. As a result of the gallery's sophisticated presentation and its thoroughly researched and comprehensive content, the National Museum of Singapore, as well as being the most technically accomplished of such institutions in the region, is also doubtless its most informative.

FROM *KAMPUNG* TO HDB

Singapore is regionally appreciated, amongst many other things, for the wealth of its period architecture. As well as the numerous grand Victorian public buildings built by the English to house their administrative personnel, the city-state boasts gracious and bucolic black-and-white bungalows and charming shophouses, today largely restored to their 19th- and early 20th-century glory. Forming the historic architectural nuclei of Chinatown, Southern Serangoon Road and other pockets dispersed around the island, these buildings provide a cachet and character that only old dwellings can. Yet, as few as 50 years ago, many of Singapore's row shophouses, now considered so picturesque, were at the heart of one of the most acute social problems facing the soon-to-be independent nation.

With Singapore's population swelling exponentially every decade due to immigration, its housing infrastructure was over capacity by the end of World War I. By the post-World War II period, due to the influx of Chinese women in the 1930s and the subsequent founding of families, the bulk of workers'— and thus the vast majority's—accommodation in Singapore consisted of a densely populated and insalubrious city-core of old shophouses, along with vast peripheral *kampung* (villages) that were either shanty slums, or, at best, provided residents with few basic amenities. To alleviate this housing shortage, the British had created the Singapore Improvement Trust (SIT) in 1927. However, the SIT was neither administratively efficient nor sufficiently motivated. And though it built Singapore's first public housing estate at Tiong Bahru—now a landmark conservation area—these flats, destined for the middle classes, were too dear for the workers who most desperately needed them.

By the time full self-governance dawned, over a third of the island's population was living in extreme squalor. Social change swiftly followed political change, and to tackle the problem, in 1960, the new government replaced the inefficient SIT with the Housing Development Board (HDB). Allotted far more power than the SIT to acquire land, demolish and construct, the HDB's basic tenet was to build massively and quickly, and make the new flats available at prices that even the poorest could afford. The programme was twofold: to build new towns on the centre's periphery to replace the squatter *kampung*, and to raze or renovate the 19th-century tenements of the central district. In 1960, the Board estimated that nearly 150,000 new homes would be needed within the decade if Singapore were to surmount her housing problem. At the time, the plan seemed absurdly ambitious, particularly for such a young, inexperienced state. Yet, through much dedication and hard work, the target was not only met but surpassed. By 1970, the HDB's satellite towns that characterise Singapore today had begun to take over the landscape.

Some *kampung* dwellers—despite the new flats' promise of running water, hygienic living conditions and modern amenities such as schools and clinics—refused to move. To them, the *kampung* presented the freedom and advantages of village life, and if water was dispensed from a single tap at the top of the lane and the risk of fire great, conversely, chickens and pigs could be kept in the yard, quite out of the question in an HDB block. To encourage people to leave, the government proposed enticingly low rents for the new flats and even provided cash incentives. Moving people out of the central shophouse slums posed other difficulties. Here, landlords, long relocated to suburban bungalows, had grown rich by packing their ramshackle properties with tenants who paid little rent. Many landlords did not consider the government compensation offered for their tenement house adequate, and many tenants, however tightly sandwiched, did not relish the idea of commuting to the centre from the satellite towns.

The majority, however, was satisfied. In the decade following Independence, nearly half of Singapore's population moved into HDB accommodation, and, today, the percentage has risen to 85 per cent, with most owning rather than renting a flat. Credited for providing housing and encouraging Singapore's social cohesion, HDB estates are today considered a global model for similar schemes in other countries.

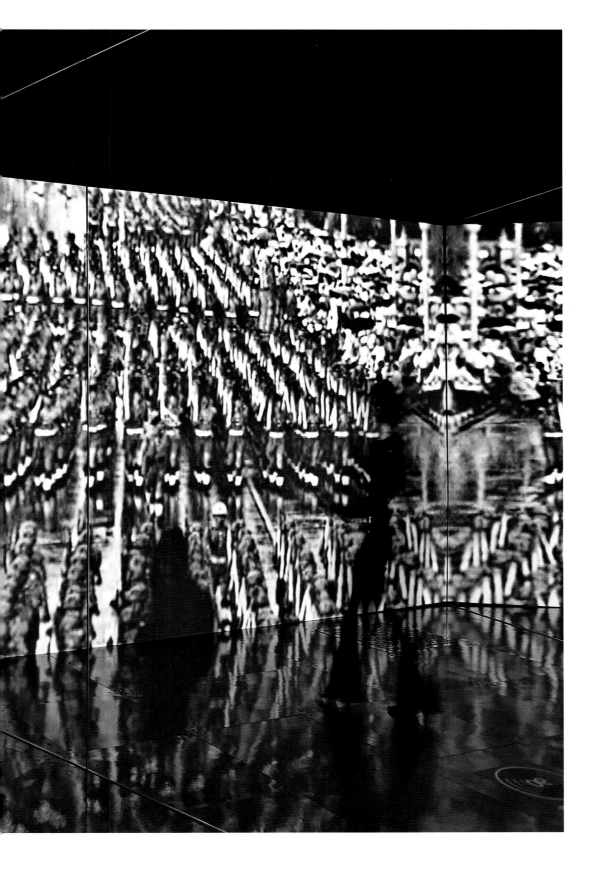

(Page 74) The wall-length
curtains of the Film Gallery
create a sense of drama.

(Below) Glove puppets and
theatre belonging to the
Sin Sai Lok troupe. Though
most puppets in the museum
collection belonged to this
Fujianese troupe that immigrated
to Singapore in the 1930s,
puppets from other parts of
China were common as well. The
painted wood theatre from the
1950s to 1960s is portable and
designed to be dismantled within
an hour. In use, its stage was lit
with over 1,000 electric bulbs,
lending performances a dazzling
and dramatic appeal.

1ocated on the east side of the Rotunda, the National Museum's Film and Wayang Gallery, is devoted to entertainment forms predominant in 20th-century Singapore before the advent of television in 1963: cinema, Chinese street opera (also known by the Malay term *wayang*) and puppetry.

The main corpus of this gallery centres on film. The motion picture was invented in Europe at the end of the 19th century, and silent films began to appear in Asia at the dawn of the new century. By the late 1920s, 'talkies', or pictures with sound, had become popular in Singapore, and some traditional performance venues such as Chinese opera houses were converting themselves into cinemas. Though the industry was initially dominated by American and European productions, home-grown studios emerged in the mid-1930s, with the Shanghai-born Shaw brothers amongst the most dynamic. Besides opening a chain of cinemas in Singapore, Malaya and the region, Shaw Brothers Pte. Ltd. began shooting Malay films in Singapore in 1937 and incorporated Malay Film Productions, known as MFP, in 1947. A second major studio, Cathay-Keris Film Productions, a partnership between producers Ho Ah Loke and Loke Wan Tho, came to the fore some 16 years later in 1953.

The first Shaw films were shot by Chinese directors, who were soon replaced by more popular Indian filmmakers. These early films generally starred Malayan actors who, working with only broadly sketched scripts, tended to improvise. The motion pictures that resulted were a hybrid of Hindi film form favouring song and dance, and Malay content, which included popular folk stories, epic tales and the *bangsawan*

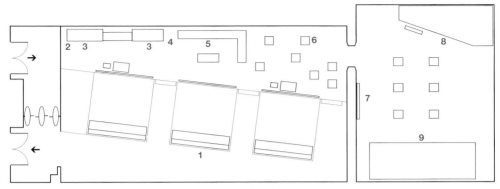

Film Gallery
1 Short Film by Royston Tan
2 Film Projector
3 Cinema Tickets and Photographs
4 Film Cases
5 Magazines and Publicity Collateral
6 Vinyl Records

Wayang (Chinese Opera) Gallery
7 Glove Puppets
8 Glove Puppet Theatre
9 Costume Showcase

(Malay opera) genre. Though production was interrupted during World War II, it resumed with vigour in the mid-1940s; in the years that followed, Indian film directors would in turn be progressively replaced by indigenous Malays. The two decades after World War II would prove to be the most productive in Singapore's filmmaking history, with Shaw Brothers and Cathay-Keris studios together launching some 260 motion pictures. However, this did not last long. Local filmmaking gradually waned in the late 1960s as political upheaval swept through the region, audience tastes changed, and television became commonplace.

The National Museum of Singapore's firm commitment to contemporary art as a means of explaining and re-actualising the past is particularly apparent in the Film and Wayang Gallery. Here, for the gallery's main section, curators have commissioned award-winning local filmmaker Royston Tan to produce a short film based on re-appropriated sequences drawn from iconic motion pictures dating mostly to the golden age of Malay cinema in the 1950s and 1960s. Using old clips as a basis for his new footage, Tan's discriminating selection and re-ordering simultaneously convey the cultural flavour of the decades leading toward and following Malayan and Singaporean national independence, while taking the films beyond their literal content.

Casting a fresh, contemporary eye on the form itself, Royston Tan breathes new life into this original but little-studied and appraised indigenous cinematographic art. The result—somewhere between document and art—pays tribute to Malayan cultural history. But beyond the filmmaker's artistic accomplishment, this institutional

he material presented in this
pace...nostalgically evokes
Singapore's culture of street
ntertainment before cinemas
ecame common here in the
ost-World War I period.

knowledgement of Singapore and Malaysia's shared
tistic wealth also obliquely recalls the National Museum
Singapore's historic 120-year old tradition of cooperation
ith Malayan cultural establishments.

Tan's six-minute film, split between three imposing
reens, combines extracts from a number of great classics,
cluding MFP's colour extravaganza *Hang Tuah* (1956),
arring the legendary Malay director, actor and singer
Ramlee; *Ribut* (1956); *Bujang Lapok* (1957); war film
atahari (1958); horror films *Sumpah Orang Minyak* (1958)
d *Anak Pontianak* (1958); *Ibu Mertuaku* (1962); and the
st Shaw film *Raja Bersiong* (1968).

Through the re-edited footage, Tan evokes not only the
nematographic culture of the day with its taste for ghost
d vampire flicks and narratives centring around a free and
ninhibited lifestyle, but perhaps, more importantly, the
ry different nature of society in pre-developed Singapore
d Malaysia. The revelation of the simplicity of life in the
ral *kampung*, with a culture based on traditional legends
d myths, will surprise many urban Singaporeans who
ould likely now consider consumerism and Islamic identity
be the two predominant societal features associated
spectively with Singapore and Malaysia today.

Didactic and entertaining, the Film and Wayang Gallery
ovides a wealth of information that camps regional
nema in its socio-political and historical context via movie
raphernalia and audiovisual presentations located behind
e large motion picture screens. Here, academics and people
volved in the film industry of the period are interviewed,
eir anecdotes, recollections and research enlightening
d expanding upon the vivid picture of mid-20th-century
alaya and Singapore drawn by Royston Tan's film.

The gallery's back room, dominated by the display of
e Fujian Sin Sai Lok troupe puppet theatre, also features

a home-movie depicting *wayang* productions, old Chinese
puppets and *wayang* costumes and accessories. Here,
several audio stations provide background information to
these more traditional entertainment forms. The material
presented in this space—and much more like it—was
brought to Singapore by the successive waves of Chinese,
Indian and Malay immigrants who came to the island in
quest of work. It nostalgically evokes Singapore's culture of
street entertainment before cinemas became common here in
the post-World War I period.

One of the gallery's largest and most spectacular artefacts
is the elaborate multi-tiered painted wood puppet theatre
belonging to the Sin Sai Lok troupe. Though built around
the 1960s, the theatre's construction, design and colourful
gilded ornamentation are all in traditional Chinese style,
and duplicate in miniature the architecture of the traditional
Chinese permanent stage. Though large, the theatre could
be dismantled and re-assembled within an hour and so was
easily installed in different parts of Singapore for the benefit
of a wide audience. As well as the stage, the majority of the
displayed glove puppets also belonged to the Sin Sai Lok
troupe that was formed in Fujian Province but was based in
Singapore from the 1930s to 1970s.

THE ART OF ROYSTON TAN

Royston Tan is often referred to as the 'bad boy' of Singapore film. Born in 1976 and educated in Singapore, he is today consider one of Singapore's more accomplished young filmmakers and directors. Tan's work featured in the museum's Film and Waya Gallery is the director's second collaboration with the museum. In 2003, Tan was commissioned by the then-Singapore Hist Museum to shoot *The Old Man and the River*, a lyrical interview-based narrative of the Singapore River and the people who liv from the waterway, made to celebrate the History Museum's three-year stint overlooking the river at Clarke Quay. Although Tan critically acclaimed outside Singapore, where he is recognised, along with his senior compatriot filmmak Eric Khoo, as part of a small Singapore cultural intelligentsia, he often regarded with mixed pride and misgivin

the city-state establishment for his honest examination of some of Singapore's less appealing social traits. In his award-
ning films, *48 on Aids* (2002) and *15* (2003), Tan realistically portrays the marginal side of Singapore society that fails to conform
and indeed, contradicts, the city-state's cultivated public image of Confucian values, along with its antiseptically clean and slick
pping malls. Articulating issues surrounding contemporary Singapore's loss of spirituality, its social conformity and substitution
consumerism for culture, Tan's films appeal to an increasingly well-informed, culturally sophisticated and critical local audience—
that is keen to make sense of identity politics and the challenges facing a budding civil society in post-nation-building Singapore.

In this latest collaboration with the National Museum of Singapore, Tan reaffirms his mastery of the art of
filmmaking, his acute eye for everyday life, and his almost uncanny knack for
capturing and portraying the distinct cultural flavours intrinsic
to Singapore and her neighbours.

Portrait of Chinese family with hand-coloured jewellery and flowers
Kwong Chow Studio, 1930s, 2000-06863

Family portrait, 1950s
Donated by Chung Kim Hua, 2002-01023

... women, 1930s-1940s

Inscribed on verso 'Given by Huang Yinye &
Gu Ji Ri to Huang Shiwei', Shanghai Studio, 1929
XX 'X 12861

Hand-coloured portrait of Peranakan Chinese couple
J. Rugdee, Penang, inscribed 30th May 1939 = 12th Day of 4th Moon, XXXX-12035

... verso 'Given by nephew Wang Youfu to
... uoshang', 1940s
... ng Chwee Seng, 1992-00181

Inscribed on verso 'Siang and siblings', 1940s
Donated by Wu Siang, 2002-00863-001

Inscribed 'Given by Chinwee & Lui to Jiangtian &
Longzhou for remembrance', November 1946
XXXX-12702

Nonya matriarch with family members, 1920s-1930s
Donated by Evelyn Ng, 1994-00061

... rait, 1950s

Group of Malay men
Ming Ngai Studio, 21 August 1947
Donated by Rosaini bte Haris, 1995-05280

Family portrait
Ciro Studio, 1960s
Donated by Mak Wai Har, 1995-20876

Angie's father (Chua Seng Soon) and friends, 1950s
Donated by Angie Chua, 2004-00845

Inscribed on verso: Nanas Timah, Art Studio, 1957
Donated by Rosaini bte Haris, 1995-05281

Studio portrait, Art Studio, April 1958
Donated by Rosaini bte Haris, 1995-05279

Angie's family friend, Ciro Studio, 1960s
Donated by Angie Chua, 2004-00852

Angie's aunt, Sun Luen Studio, 1950s
Donated by Angie Chua, 2004-00840

Angie's cousin (Siew Yuen), Sun Luen Studio, 1960s
Donated by Angie Chua, 2004-00838

Angie's cousin (Siew Yuen), Sun Luen Studio, 1960s
Donated by Angie Chua, 2004-00837

Inscribed on verso: Given by Qian Zhanhui, Zhaoqing &
Fengping to Mak Guequ for remembrance, 1961
Donated by Chen Chia Hong, 1995-00877

Angie's family friends, Ciro Studio, 1950s
Donated by Angie Chua, 2004-00851

Inscribed on verso: Ang Chwee Seng second from right
1940-1950s, Donated by Ang Khoon Seng, 1992-00141

Two young girls, Adeff Studio, 1950s
Donated by Ang Chwee Seng, 1992-00140

Family portrait, 1940s-1950s
1000-10405

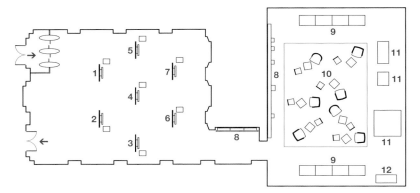

1 Guess Who's Coming for Dinner
2 Sending a Letter Home
3 Keeping It Together
4 The Black and White Amahs
5 Marrying within the Community
6 Polygamy in Singapore
7 Settling Down in Singapore
8 The Promenade
9 Walls of Drawers
10 Family Albums
11 A Showcase of Photographic Equipment
12 Family and Friends: A Singapore Album Database

also located on the Rotunda's east side, the Photo Gallery examines the development of the family over the last hundred years. Here, visitors explore various sociological themes conjured by seven enlarged black-and-white digital images made from original portrait negatives taken from the collections of the National Museum and National Archives of Singapore. These images are presented in tandem with seven audiovisual shorts, screened on interactive television monitors backing each photograph. The films combine text, audio and visual information to provide a sharp, snapshot view of their subject. Text captions impart historical information in accessible, anecdotal form. Soundtracks, for their part, incorporate scripts drawn from interviews and academic research. Visual material includes enacted sequences, contemporary filmed interviews with Singaporeans, and archival photographs taken by amateurs and professional photographic studios.

If the medium is approachable, the subjects touched upon in this gallery are far from frivolous, some of them indeed figuring amongst the most socio-politically significant of their day. The topic of interracial marriage

(Page 82) A section of the Promenade in the gallery's Back Room, featuring Singapore photo studio portraits of families and individuals recorded in the course of the 20th century.

(Below) Through its presentation of local studio portraits taken from the late 19th century to the 1970s, the gallery's Front Room explores a century of evolving family history in Singapore.

(Below) Featuring antique-style
Chinese furniture, the Back
Room is where visitors may
comfortably peruse family
albums reproduced from original
photographs in the National
Museum of Singapore collection.
1960s' studio equipment from
the Tong Lam Photo Studio is
visible in the background.

(Opposite) A view of a computer
terminal where the national
archival project *Family and
Friends: A Singapore Album*
database may be viewed.
The site includes a selection
of documented and digitised
photographs of Singapore
individuals, families or
community groups.

is broached via an 1890s photograph of a Turkish woman wedded to the Sultan of Johore and splendidly dressed in the most hybrid of high Victorian gowns made entirely of indigenous gold-embroidered *songket* (luxurious brocade from Indonesia or peninsular Malaysia with a silk or cotton ground and gold woven thread). Though commonplace in the early 21st century, mixed marriages were still something of a taboo in Singapore during the 1970s. Here, this socially thorny issue is given depth and meaning by an interview with a Chinese-Australian couple who wed in the 1960s. Stretching to just over seven minutes, the piece, empathy-creating and human, succeeds in imparting a great deal of information relating to custom and expectations in domestic life 30 years ago. Gender roles in the family context, equality of the sexes, and the structure and lifestyle of the Chinese extended family are examples of themes that the film clip explores in a matter-of-fact, articulate way.

An enacted film clip, inspired by a 1910 photograp of two *karayuki-san* (Japanese prostitutes), describes th life of Japanese sex workers in Singapore at the turn the last century. Through a fictitious letter written to h brother in Japan, a young prostitute candidly describe the hardship-filled and solitary life she leads in the colon In viewing this, the observant museum-goer will catc a glimpse of early Singapore. He gleans that life for th migrant labourers in the colony, who dreamt of returnin home rich but seldom did, was an extremely lonely one f lack of female companions from their home countries; understands that the community of prostitutes in Singapo was probably fairly cosmopolitan; and, finally, he ascertai from the Japanese lady's frank and honest description of h work that she is not at all ashamed to be earning a livir from her body, that being the only livelihood open to he Though the film clip does not underscore this aspect, mar

isitors, particularly those from Western ountries, will be fascinated to note the lear absence of moral stigma attached o the oldest profession here, in likely ontrast with the prudish and censorious ttitudes pervasive in contemporary dwardian England.

Another of the gallery's seven key mages is a black-and-white photograph from the 1920s or 930s, this time depicting a Chinese family. Quite well to do, he young patriarch and his eight children wear European lothes while his two wives sport the *cheongsam*, a traditional hinese dress. Polygamy is the topic here, and the short lm behind the photograph goes a long way to elucidating practice that was only outlawed in Singapore's Chinese ommunity in 1961 by the first fully elected government.

A fourth photograph portrays a Chinese working-lass wedding held in 1936. The image explains what few oday would suspect: that, except for European women n Singapore with their colonist spouses, a few well-off Jyonyas (Peranakan or Straits Chinese women whose ulture is part Malay, part Chinese) wedded to wealthy hinese businessmen, and prostitutes from the region and eyond, very few women, and fewer still Asian women, nade their home in Singapore until the 1930s. Only after the reat Depression of 1929 did women begin to leave Southern hina and arrive in the Straits Settlements in any quantity. ut, contrary to what one might expect, they travelled here ot because summoned by their men-folk but because they ought work to escape increasing hardship and poverty at ome. They too took labourer jobs and, having toiled in he fields of China, could well manage the construction site nd port-hauling work of Singapore. It is only when these newly-arrived women began founding families with their male compatriots already installed here that the family, as a an-society institution (as opposed to the relatively few elite Peranakan families), truly took root in Singapore.

The Peranakan Babas (Peranakan or Straits Chinese men whose culture is part Chinese, part Malay) had no such lifficulty finding brides. Generally established in peninsular Malaya before moving south to Singapore, these Chinese merchants, unlike their labourer co-nationals, generally had no intention of returning to China and so sought indigenous wives. The 1912 photograph of the compact Peranakan family shown in the gallery gives many clues to the hybridity of local culture at the turn of the last century. The father wears a Chinese silk brocade jacket, revealing his attachment to ancestral custom. However, he sports a *sarong* (garment consisting of a length of fabric worn around the waist by men and women of Indonesia, peninsular Malaysia and other Southeast Asian countries), perhaps a concession to comfort in the tropical heat. While the children are dressed in European style—Peranakan children were often educated in Western-run missionary schools and would later possibly join the colonial civil service—the wife is covered head to toe in a heavy Chinese-style embroidered silk *baju panjang* (long tunic with a sarong), her outfit combining fabric that appeals to the Chinese with a Malay form of dress.

Other photographs featured in the main part of the gallery include a 1910 cliché of European children in the company of their Chinese *amah* (nanny or wet nurse), and a 1914 Armenian bridal party. Both images recall Singapore's cosmopolitan identity even a century ago.

The gallery's Back Room, designed as a cross between a photographer's waiting room and a family living room, presents vintage photographic equipment and hundreds of old photographs of Singapore and her residents. Rotated periodically, the photos emphasise the trading centre's cosmopolitan nature, its population shown here to include many nationalities and ethnic representatives. Some sepia images are displayed in facsimile family photo albums that can be consulted while sitting on faux-antique Chinese furniture, as if in a friend's living room. One of the earliest images of Singapore in the daguerreotype format, taken by a visiting French official in 1844, is also on view here in one of the specially-designed light-controlled drawer showcases.

Through innovative use of multimedia and archival photographic material, the National Museum charts facets of the nation's domestic history from a small number of personal stories. With the help of contemporary technology and thoughtful design strategy, socially significant concerns of the past, however remote, are brought vividly to life so that they have meaning and relevance to audiences today.

THE EARLIEST PHOTOGRAPH OF SINGAPORE

The earliest known photographic image of Singapore is the *Daguerreotype of Singapore Town* by Frenchman Alphonse-Eugène-Jules Itier. Now housed in the National Museum of Singapore collection, the plate was produced in 1844, five years after Itier's compatriot Louis-Jacques-Mandé Daguerre invented what later became known as the daguerreotype technique of permanent photographic reproduction.

The daguerreotype view of Singapore shown in the museum is believed to be one of four taken by Itier, a Customs Service officer working in Asia on behalf of the French Government. On a tour of duty as the head of a trade mission to Southeast Asia and China, Itier arrived in the Straits Settlement in July 1844. Though naturally impressed by the island's attractive landscape, tropical flora and small but cosmopolitan population, Itier was most seduced by Singapore's bustling free-trading port.

Eager to keep a record of the port's commercial dynamism, and its colourful mix of international traders and vessels hailing from the four corners of the globe, Itier set up his equipment on the crest of Government Hill, present-day Fort Canning Hill. The tools of the trade of early photographers such as Itier would have consisted of a silver-coated copper plate for recording the image, assorted chemicals—including extremely toxic, heated mercury—and a curtained black box on legs for exposing the plate.

At the top of Fort Canning, through his primitive camera's viewfinder, Itier would have observed what many visiting European topographical artists recording Singapore before him had seen: a classical port and river scene. Alphonse-Eugène-Jules Itier, however, as one of Europe's pioneers of the new daguerreotype, with the immediacy, precision and rawness unique to the medium of photography, captured with his single irreproducible plate, the drive and naked ambition of mid-19th-century Singapore in a way that no artist wielding brush or pen could.

Actual view of Singapore Town

Daguerreotype of Singapore Town
Alphonse-Eugène-Jules Itier
1844–1845
Silver-coated copper plate

This is one of the four earliest photographic images made of Singapore, just five years after Louis Daguerre invented this process in France. The daguerreotype, popular from the early 1840s to the 1850s, was one of the first commercially used processes to record a permanent but laterally reversed image. It is identified by its highly polished silver surfaces and by the fact that at different viewing angles, the image appears either as a positive or a negative.

This daguerreotype was taken from Government Hill (present-day Fort Canning) by Alphonse-Eugène-Jules Itier, a French Customs Service officer who was impressed by the commercial buzz in Singapore. This scene was a classic landmark view often sketched and painted by visiting European artists in the 19th century.

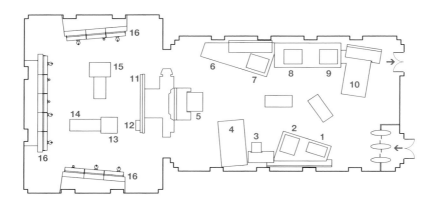

1 Laksa	7 Sarabat	12 Kopi Tiam
2 Char Kway Teow	8 Bak Kut Teh	13 Coconut Graters
3 Tok-tok Mee	9 Hainanese	14 Mortars and Pestles
4 Kueh Tutu	Chicken Rice	15 Kitchen
5 Roti Prata	10 Satay	Curiosities
6 Nasi Lemak	11 Cake Moulds	16 Wall of Spices

Whatever their ethnic origin, income or political slant might be, most, if not all, Singaporeans would agree on the importance of food. One of the most diverse cuisines in the world, local gastronomy, characterised by its fusion of the tastes of Singapore's diverse cultures brought to the island by her many peoples, provides a unique key to unlocking the complexity of the nation's layered history.

The Food Gallery focuses as much on the nature of local cuisine as on its mode of preparation and most common distribution venue: the street. Indeed, Singapore, though now a developed and prosperous nation, still today claims one of the most important street-food cultures—perhaps the very largest per capita—in the world. But beyond the hybridity of local recipes, attesting to the influence of regional Chinese, Malay, South and North Indian, and Portuguese cuisine amongst others, Singapore's street food is revealing of social patterns and paths of economic development quite unique to the island.

Certainly, street food inspired by popular taste is common all over Asia. Hawker stalls and itinerant food vendors are, however, a particularity of pre-Independence Malaya and Singapore because their obligatory presence poignantly reflected the needs of the majority of the peninsula's Asian migrant population that consisted virtually only of single men until well after the beginning of the 20th century. Until the 1930s, when women began arriving in Singapore en masse, the impoverished Chinese, Indian and Malay labourers who streamed onto the island to find work had no one at home to cook for them. Mostly packed into the squalid accommodation of the central district's old shophouses, these workers were barely supplied sleeping space, let alone

(Page 90) A display of 70 foods and spices used in the Southeast Asian kitchen. The line-up of glass jars is visually appealing and reminiscent of a science lab, reminding museum-goers of local dishes' myriad origins.

(Above) The sociology of food is explored through artefact and photographic displays as well as multimedia presentations capturing the environment of a lively street filled with itinerant food vendors and hawker stalls.

itchen facilities. Further, life in Singapore for many of iem was viewed as temporary and until the 1930s, when ie influx of women prompted them to found families, there as little concept of making the island home. Cheap street od therefore served a practical purpose as well as reflected ie precarious nature of existence in the migrant colony.

These days, street food is no longer a necessity mirroring arsh socioeconomic realities. However, in Singapore, the assion for it remains, hybrid hawker fare material proof of ingaporeans' openness to diverse culture and customs.

Comprising two rooms, the Food Gallery narrates ingapore sociology through food using state-of-the-art iultimedia, multi-sensory and interactive strategies along ith artefact-based and photographic displays. Well-esearched oral histories, telling of real people's experiences the street food business, also play a key role. The Gallery's ain area references a street setting where different hawkers

congregate selling their fare. Displays focus on 10 different Singapore specialities: chicken rice, *laksa* (noodles in coconut soup), *char kway teow* (fried flat noodles), *tok-tok mee* (noodles), *roti prata* (flat fried bread with curry), *sarabat* (a ginger drink, although sarabat stalls sold all types of drinks), *nasi lemak* (rice cooked in coconut milk), *satay* (grilled meat on a stick), *bak kut teh* (pork bone soup) and *kueh tutu* (steamed cake). The dishes' composition and confection are explained and often filmed, giving even the hurried visitor an immediate and accurate idea of Singapore's ethnic make-up as well as the sense of Singapore as an international port-city where every possible sort of spice was available.

Because of the difficulty of finding older equipment and witnesses, the material exhibits and taped audio accounts documenting the dishes and hawkers' past way of life tend to date to Singapore's post-Independence decades of the 1960s and 1970s. Yet, despite the relative youth of the artefacts—a

94

(Below) Here, visitors familiarise themselves with the aroma of spices used in local cuisine through a smell-device fitted into the gallery wall. The device, which resembles a showerhead, hides a tiny jar filled with spice essence concocted by Givaudan Singapore Pte Ltd.

(Opposite) Foods, spices and herbs are displayed either in freeze-dried form, or as a replica if easily perishable. Reproductions of 19th-century prints illustrate local dishes' components; the latter's unique qualities and use in Southeast Asian cooking are also featured.

Flower crab

Flower crabs (known as *ketam pasir* or 'sand crabs' in Malay), die soon after they are caught and taken out of the water, and their flesh deteriorates quickly. If cooked soon after being caught, they have a sweet, firm texture and are more delicate than mud crabs. There are three different styles of cooking them; all with equally delicious results: South Indian curry, Peranakan Chinese curry, and steamed in the Chinese way.

ueh tutu seller's stand mounted on an old bicycle with parasol, and an itinerant *satay* vendor's portable stall equipment, which include squat spartan wooden stools, enamel pots, kerosene lamp, iron *satay* holder, and bamboo *kander* pole for carrying the stall across the shoulders—they might well be from the turn of the last century, so different was life in the 1970s compared to conditions merely three decades later.

The room's sound-design, by Darren Ng, conveys the street in all its cacophony, the gallery resounding with the multilingual cries of hawkers, the clanging of cooking utensils, the sizzling purr of hot oil frying, the pounding of spices in the traditional stone mortar and, finally, the hawkers' announcement of their specialities with the persistent 'tok-tok' of bamboo hitting bamboo. Signalling the different versions of *mee*, this nearly musical knocking is familiar to all Singaporeans who remember the noodle vendors' signature call.

Various audiovisual stations provide documentaries showcasing oral histories aired with archival photographs, and short films (from director Victric Thng) on demand. Though concise and anecdotal, these prove both visually compelling and historically enlightening. A North Indian *parabat* vendor who worked for the British recalls how including European sandwiches in his menu made his mobile stand so well-presented that 'even whites were amongst his clients'. Validating the museum's testimony-based approach to history, this single, offhand comment from a participant—rather than an observer—of the island's history says much about race segregation in mid-20th century Singapore.

A Chinese man remembers life in Bugis street in the 1950s when office staff would patronise the food stalls after work and, once gone, would be replaced by a second wave of patrons: a far rowdier crowd that included British sailors, and well-off local business men and their fancy girls. As well as giving visitors a taste of Singapore's red light district of the period, this testimony at the same time obliquely alludes to the fact that the British did not withdraw their military presence from Singapore until the 1970s.

A third account, this time narrated by a Malay stallholder, recalls the interviewee's childhood helping her mother prepare and serve *nasi lemak*. Homey and colloquial, the story reveals the life experienced by the woman and her family in one of Singapore's many rural *kampung,* now long gone. The clip also speaks of the many poor factory workers who bought food at her family's stand, thus recalling Singapore's industrialising past. Further, the story underscores entrepreneurship, even on a small scale, as a common and much relied upon means of lifting Singapore migrant families out of extreme poverty. Finally, the woman, who is of Indonesian origin, in her very appearance on camera affords some significant historical insight into the evolution of religious custom in Singapore and the region: while in the old photographs of her family, neither she, her sister nor her mother wears the Muslim head scarf, on film in 2006, her head is completely covered.

Other types of short films inspired by scenes from old Singapore—one depicting an itinerant noodle-seller hoisting steaming bowls of *mee pok* (flat noodles) to a lady client through her shophouse window is particularly charming—provide telling illustrations of the personalised relationship between hawker and customer in the days before centralised hawker centres were instituted in the post-war period. Through these parochial accounts, gallery visitors connect with the past through a combination of identification, nostalgia and discovery of forgotten custom.

A second room at the gallery's rear provides a playful and hands-on experience for visitors striving to learn more about the island's cuisine. Here, the myriad spices, herbs and other ingredients common in Singapore gastronomy line the walls in jars where they can not only be seen, but also smelled. Cooking equipment from the past is also featured, as is a series of colourful and coarse ceramic *kopi tiam* (coffee shop) cups and saucers. The latter, dating from the days when Singaporeans congregated in local coffee shops rather than in today's foreign-owned chains, is a small but nostalgia-filled star display that is bound to touch older locals.

SOCIOLOGY THROUGH FOOD

The hawker fare that Singapore is famous for is prepared and eaten on the street because traditionally, neither those cooking nor those consuming the food could afford a dedicated restaurant-style venue. Four hawker specialities that speak volumes about Singapore's multi-ethnic, multicultural peoples and their history are *laksa*, *roti prata*, *char kway teow* and *satay*.

The soupy Peranakan mainstay, *laksa*, is a good example of the Straits' and Singapore's distinct cultural mix. A hybrid combination of Malay and Southern Chinese culinary traditions, the rice noodle and coconut milk-based *laksa* is an indigenous favourite that was born when the migrant Chinese combined their noodles with the indigenous Malays' coconut and spices. Even the dish's name, coming from the Persian *laksha* (noodle) and thus attesting to the presence of Persian traders in early Malacca where the speciality was born, underscores its cosmopolitan heritage.

Another indigenous speciality, *char kway teow*, is a high-fat, high-carbohydrate dish of stir-fried flat rice noodles that was first prepared by local fishermen, farmers and cockle gatherers keen to make extra money by catering to hungry but impoverished labourers returning from their day shift. High in calories, the dish was an inexpensive source of energy for coolies who could afford little else for their meals. As a subsistence food of the poor, *char kway teow* was served on palm leaves by night hawkers; as well as being free, this also contributed to the dish's flavour. Till this day, *char kway teow* remains a Singapore night market favourite.

Roti prata (yeastless bread) is a typically Singaporean cross-cultural dish traditionally sold by South Indian Muslim men. The indigenous touch comes from its method of preparation since, rather than served plain, as it might be in India, the flattened unleavened bread is in Singapore fried in *ghee* (Indian clarified butter) on a cast-iron griddle and eaten with curry.

The term 'satay' comes from the Tamil word for flesh (*sathai*) and refers to grilled spice-marinated chicken, lamb or beef enjoyed in Singapore, Malaysia and Indonesia. The method for grilled marinated meat probably travelled to Southeast Asia by way of India, certainly coming initially from the Middle East. However, the addition of lemongrass and tamarind to the marinade concoction, and the kebabs' pairing with *ketupat* (Malay compressed rice cakes) and chilli-peanut sauce (its South American ingredients were originally brought to the Malay Peninsula and the Indonesian archipelago by the Portuguese in the 17th century), lend this popular dish a cosmopolitan flavour like no other. A food reflecting the itinerant lifestyle of the region's migrant people, *satay* was prepared in portable stalls that could be packed up and suspended from a shoulder-borne carrying pole.

(Page 98) Popular fabrics from the 1950s to 1970s located in the Sewing Room at the rear of the Fashion Gallery.

(Below) The Music Booths feature 1960s' rock and roll by Singapore's own bands and interviews with Singaporeans relating to the period.

(Right) The Sewing Room presents visitors to the Fashion Gallery with a showcase of colours and textures.

this gallery, on the west side of the old wing, narrates Singaporean, and, more specifically, Singaporean women's, social history through fashion. Focusing on the era spanning the 1950s to the 1970s, it dissects the major and unprecedented social changes during these key decades as Singapore passed from colonial rule to its new status as a politically independent republic. Through displays of clothes, accessories and beauty products, popular culture is used to comment on the nation as its economy grew from pre-industrial to developed, and as its women assumed their share of responsibility in shaping these developments.

Music too plays an important role in setting the period stage and, like the clothing of the day, was at that time only recently westward-looking. Through a combination of exhibits featuring women's clothing from the mid century to early 1970s, and audiovisual clips highlighting in newsreel documentary form the great events of the period of particular relevance to women, visitors get a sense of the momentous changes that were visited on the women of Singapore in the second half of the 20th century. The information, presented by decade, is not truly limited to the post-war period and gallery-goers are reminded that in 1900, most women living here were Western and the

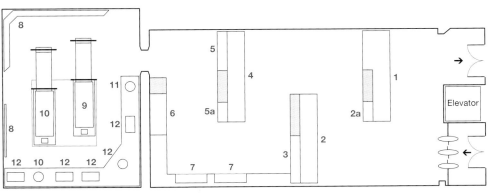

1 Silhouettes
2 Cosmopolitanism
2a Cheongsam and Accessories
3 Costumes and Wigs
4 Modesty and Notions of Beauty

5 Youth Culture
5a Trouser Suit and Accessories
6 First Ladies
7 Music Interactives
8 Fabrics, Patterns and Motifs

9   Making a Kebaya
10 Making a Cheongsam
11 Draping a Sari
12 Sewing Machines and
    Wedding Gown

most Asian girls only began being educated after World War II. Bullet-style information clips, accompanied by pop music of the day, announce the events—many political—harbouring the greatest sociological impact of the decade. The promulgation of the Women's Charter in 1961 doubtless contributed to Singaporean women's emancipation and entry into the workforce. And though the gallery wallboards do not elaborate this point, the implied consequences of some 20 per cent more people contributing their skills and effort to the local economy goes far to explaining the extraordinarily fast pace of economic development in post-Independence Singapore. Women, more than passive witnesses to Singapore's story of progress, were actively involved in that progress. Other significant milestones of the day include the outlawing of polygamy in 1961 and the government's adoption of an official population policy in the late 1960s that, on a practical level, was indispensable to Singaporean women in their quest for full equality.

If the clothes on view in the Fashion Gallery are evidence of an opening of Singapore society to Western modernity, as well as the development of a truly Singaporean identity further to active nation-building in the years immediately after Independence, then the popular music of the times proposes a slightly different outlook on the same period. Through interviews available at two audio stations, visitors hear of the clash between local youth, interested in Western pop and rock music, and more conservative elements of society—namely, the government—keen to keep what was perceived as lax, decadent Western mores out of Singapore.

Curators, providing a balanced account of history, aired interviews with a former government official, How Mun Seng, Assistant Secretary to the Ministry of Home Affairs in the 1970s, and with a local radio deejay of the period. Needless to say, their respective points of view on sexuality and youth culture are quite different. From their differing opinions, a generation that has grown up in a much freer, more open and prosperous Singapore gets a realistic and non-glorified taste of the past. The seemingly trivial subject of hair length is viewed from both sides of the societal divide, the civil servant equating long hair with drug abuse, and the deejay adopting a more liberal stance. Government and radio censorship of 1970s' air waves programming is evoked in a straightforward manner that in some cases still eludes Singapore's mainstream media today, the museum examining this sensitive subject with an even-handed approach.

Another issue brought to the fore by one of the interviews is Singapore's culture of substitution in the realm of popular music. In the 1960s and 1970s, the young were so desperate for Western pop groups, which so seldom made it to the island in the flesh, that indigenous bands sought to imitate the foreigners. The closer to the original in sound, style and look, the more successful was the copycat band. Visitors are left to draw their own conclusions from the information but, again, the approach to history here is not just accessible, but both intelligent and thought-provoking.

Beyond the main body of the gallery, an area known as the Sewing Room displays the many types of fabric used by Singapore women to confect garments in the 1950s '60s and '70s, from traditional cottons and silks, to the synthetics available from the 1960s. Also featured are old sewing machines, as well as one of the stars of the museum's clothing collection: a Sylvia Kho wedding gown.

Interactive and engaging, the Fashion Gallery necessarily appeals to all because whatever one's background, one cannot fail to be immersed to a certain degree in the most pervasive aspects of popular culture: fashion and music. However, beyond providing a nostalgic trip down memory lane, the Fashion Gallery brings some salient but little-studied historical cultural truths to the fore that would warrant greater academic attention.

...beyond providing a nostalgic trip down memory lane, the Fashion Gallery brings some salient but little-studied historical cultural truths to the fore that would warrant greater academic attention.

(Opposite) Trouser suit and accessories from the 1970s.

(Below) Early 1960s' Western garments on display against an audiovisual projection that conveys Singapore's social, economic and political context from the 1940s to the 1970s.

SINGAPORE'S PIONEER WOMAN ENTREPRENEUR SYLVIA KHO

Sylvia Kho is widely considered Singapore's first fashion icon. Born Wong Sen Moy in early 20th-century Kuala Lumpur to a Chinese tin and rubber industrialist father, Kho demonstrated an interest in sewing and design before she was an adolescent. She was first taught dressmaking and beading skills by her Peranakan mother, and later studied beauty and design in America and Europe before returning to Singapore in 1946 to start her own business. Initially receiving her female clientele in her MacPherson home, Kho, in those post-war years, conducted cooking, sewing and beauty classes, as well as tailored high-end designs for her patrons.

Her reputation grew, and soon, elaborate wedding gowns, one of which is housed in the Fashion Gallery, were being commissioned by the local elite. Unlike traditional dressmakers who had never left Singapore, Kho, beyond offering her customers bespoke tailoring, also provided the sophistication of up-to-date Western styles and elegant, often foreign-sourced, fabrics. Good quality European clothing was not commonly imported into Singapore at the time, so Kho's service, and the cosmopolitan chic look she guaranteed, were very much sought after.

By the 1960s, Kho had begun selling full wedding packages to accompany her dresses. Flower arrangements, make-up and hairstyling were all custom-designed for her clients, lending their wedding a distinctive and personalised cachet. Singapore's brides could not get enough of Kho's unique brand of style and practicality, and business flourished. By the early 1970s, Kho had opened two salons from where she sold and rented wedding gowns and organised prenuptial services such as hairdressing.

Kho's client base consisted mainly of Singapore and the region's elite, including the royalty of Brunei and Malaysia. However, less well-to-do families also patronised Sylvia Kho, who is well-remembered for her generosity toward brides who could not afford her gowns and so were given them. Sylvia Kho retired from her business in the mid-1990s but her pioneering legacy of entrepreneurial innovation and style continues to inspire young Singaporeans today.

FASHION AS A BAROMETER OF SOCIO-POLITICAL CHANG

The Fashion Gallery provides a survey of vestimentary custom in the years leading up to and following Singapore's independence. After World War II, the island opened progressively to the West, turning its gaze toward more westernised Asian cities such as Tokyo and Hong Kong. With the influx of magazines from fashion capitals, including New York and Paris, Asian women, of whom there were now significantly more (men, until the 1930s, were in the majority), became aware of the apparel choices available to them beyond the traditional clothing they had grown up with. Increasingly educated, with some entering the workforce, these women embraced Western fashion for its novelty, practicality, and signalling of emancipation and progress.

The slim, elongated lines of mid-century European fashion and the tight-waisted, full skirts of Paris' New Look in the late 1950s made their way to Singapore, where women either wore the foreign designs as they came, or fused some of these new elements with traditional styles to obtain a hybrid garment. Furthermore, although the educated classes had always mixed, it was only at this time that exchange between members of different ethnic communities was becoming commonplace in all social strata. Local fashions thus reflected this social integration, with, for example, fabrics indigenous to one culture being sewn up into the national dress of another.

In the 1960s, rapidly industrialising Singapore emerged as a new Asian centre for the production of textiles. This again changed the local fashion scene since the textiles, largely destined for export, were designed to Western specification and influenced local taste.

At this time, too, cheap synthetics were being imported from Kor and Japan, offering even less well-off women the opportunity sew an alternative to traditional dress.

The fashion choices made by Singapore's First Ladies the tumultuous and politically crucial decades that follow Independence are of particular relevance. Indeed, clothes this era reflect not only a society-wide growing awareness the subtle balance of ethnic and cultural allegiances, but al the knowledge that clothing could make a political statement articulating a nationalistic bias.

Puan Noor Aishah, the wife of self-governing Singapore's fi non-European head of state Yusof Ishak (1959–1970), chose I public wardrobe in accordance with political sentiment of t time. The recent independence of then-Malaya—which join with Singapore, Sabah and Sarawak to form Malaysia from 19 to 1965—and Indonesia prompted the political elite to adopt overtly Malayan form of dress that included the *kebaya pendek* short *kebaya*, the *kebaya* being a woman's long-sleeved, ope necked fitted top favoured by Javanese Peranakan wome and women in peninsular Malaysia), the *baju panjang* and t *kain panjang* (a garment for ceremonial occasions resembling *sarong*, but made from longer cloth and not sewn into a tube).

Singapore's next First Lady, Yeo Seh Geok, wife of Preside Benjamin Sheares (1971–1981), espoused a modernised Chine style of dress that featured the *cheongsam* (a long, form-fitti traditional Chinese dress with a high collar and slit skirt).

other spaces

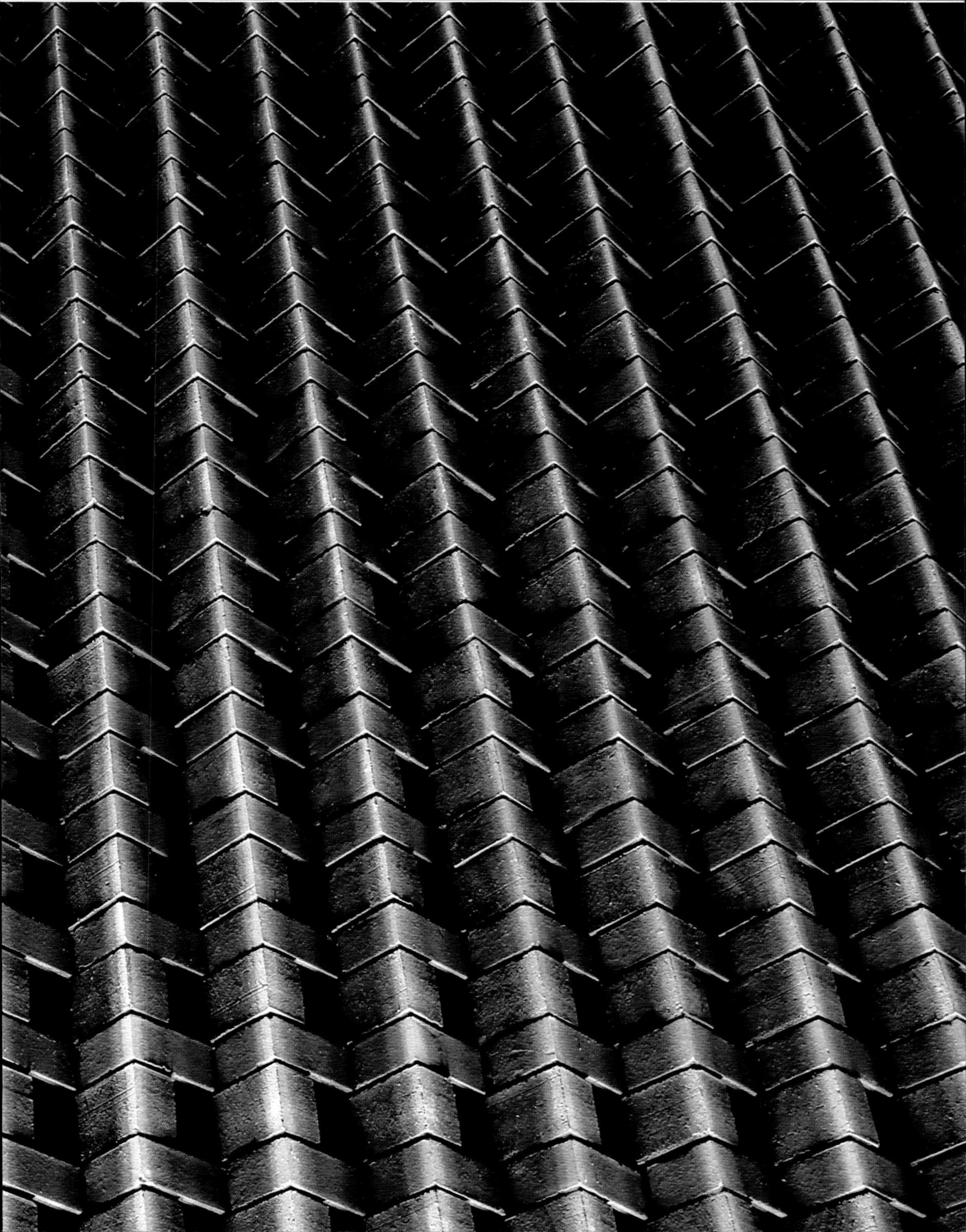

as well as the Living and History Galleries, the National Museum of Singapore houses a number of auxiliary spaces. These are crucial both to Singapore and the institution—increasing the city-state's ability to host major art exhibitions of all types, and helping the museum in its ambition to act as a living laboratory for the presentation and development of new art forms emerging from traditional performance, dance, music and other media.

The larger non-permanent gallery spaces are located in the museum's Canyon basement, dug out of Fort Canning Hill. They include the Gallery Theatre and the expansiv Exhibition Galleries 1 and 2. Other more specialised spaces— the Education Centre with The Lab and The Atelier—a located above the Atrium on the museum's top floor adjacer to the building's Fort Canning Hill entrance.

The museum's most frequently visited ancillary local are the two Exhibition Galleries and the Gallery Theatr The Exhibition Galleries, entirely column-free and boastin a soaring 6-metre-high ceiling, cover just under 1,200 squa metres, and constitute one of the city's largest and mo technologically versatile exhibition spaces. Cavernous an fitted with state-of-the-art electronic facilities enabling th

(Page 108) The Gallery Theatre's brick-clad soundproof wall.

(Above, left) View of one of the basement's two temporary Exhibition Galleries.

(Above, right) Spacious and technologically versatile, the Exhibition Galleries are ideal for all kinds of art displays and audiovisual installations.

...increasing the city-state's ability to host major art exhibitions of all types, and helping the museum in its ambition to act as a living laboratory for the presentation and development of new art forms...

(Left) View of the Gallery Theatre from its control room.

(Below) The Gallery Theatre is not only a performing arts space for theatre, dance and music performances, but can also be converted into a cinémathèque.

display of audiovisual installations, the rooms are particularly well-suited to showcase overscale three-dimensional works of art as well as technologically sophisticated new media forms. Imposing pieces make their way into the galleries from outside the building through an extra-large entrance bay, and the galleries, separated by a sliding partition such that they can operate either as two individual spaces or a single larger area, can bear loads of up to several tonnes.

Selected as a key venue for Singapore Biennale 2006, the city's inaugural international biennale of contemporary art, held from September to November 2006, the National Museum introduced its two galleries to the public, amongst other areas in the museum, several months before its official opening in December 2006. Due to their impressive size, unobstructed expanse, and ability to accommodate every possible type of art, these two unique gallery spaces have eliminated the spatial and environmental constraints that previously handicapped the city, enhancing the museum's credibility as a host of major international art events.

The Gallery Theatre is adjacent to the Exhibition Galleries. With 247 seats, the theatre or sometimes-cinema provides an intimate arena perfectly proportioned for the appreciation of live performance. The Gallery Theatre is a key venue for the presentation of varied and vibrant festivals and events designed to nurture new creative possibilities in culture and heritage. Past performances staged here have shown how the flavour of a traditional dance or theatrical work can be captured by a contemporary piece using innovative performance techniques. Equipped with the latest digital surround sound, projection systems, and movable seating, the Gallery Theatre also plays host to the National Museum of Singapore's cinémathèque programmes and other external media initiatives, such as the Singapore International Film Festival.

The Gallery Theatre is a key venue for the presentation of varied and vibrant festivals and events designed to nurture new creative possibilities in culture and heritage.

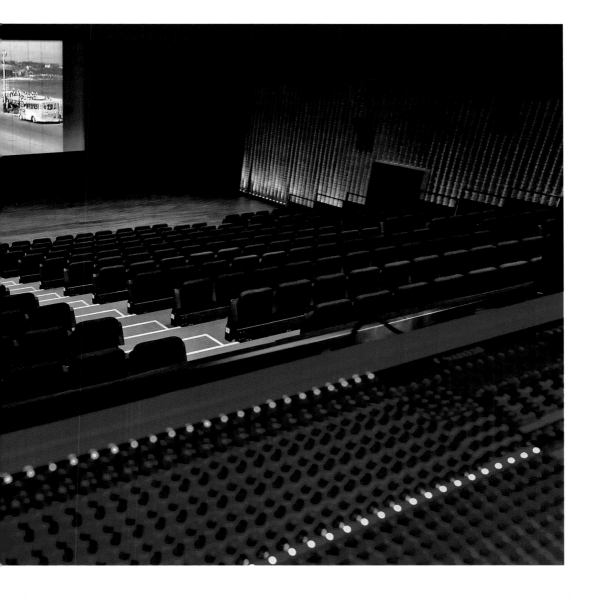

(Left) The elegant minimalist staircase leading to the Education Centre.

(Opposite) A view of the National Museum of Singapore restaurant—Novus. Serving refined European cuisine, Novus offers elegant dining inside the old part of the museum and within the institution's landscaped inner courtyard.

...a lightweight floating effect, with the Education Centre seemingly hovering, unsupported, above the Atrium's glass roof, thus visually underscoring the overall light-filled and airy feel of the new annexe.

The Gallery Theatre is located precisely in the area once occupied by the car park of the now-razed old National Library building. A significant and much-loved and frequented cultural landmark from 1960 until its demolition in 2004, the old library remains with us in spirit, the Gallery Theatre's brick-clad walls providing an apt visual reference to the memory of the modernist red-brick library. The theatre's cocoon-like interior, dominated by the warm terracotta hues of its walls, fulfils acoustic as well as aesthetic exigencies since the bricks, meticulously laid out in a herringbone pattern, encourage sound to travel beyond them to a special noise-absorbing buffer located behind the theatre walls. When designers and architects were conceiving the 2006 annexe, it was suggested that bricks from the demolished Stamford Road library be salvaged and re-used in the new theatre's construction. However, the plan was abandoned due to its prohibitive cost and the difficulty posed by the sorting and cleaning of the old bricks.

The Education Centre, camped at the museum's summit, by its rear Fort Canning Hill entrance, was designed specifically to sit on a single point of support atop the Atrium's Visitor Services Counter. The architectural concept aims to achieve a lightweight floating effect, with the Education Centre seemingly hovering, unsupported, above the Atrium's glass roof, thus visually underscoring the overall light-filled and airy feel of the new annexe. Cantilevered some 10 metres above the Visitor Services Counter, the Education Centre appears to defy gravity, acting as an aesthetic foil for the dark stone surface of the museum floor and rear driveway area. The Centre, also called 'The Mesh' because of the champagne-coloured punctured cladding surrounding its elongated box-like structure, houses various zones dedicated to the museum's many educational and lifestyle programmes.

Two sub-areas of the Education Centre are The Lab and The Atelier. The Lab is the museum's main venue for workshops. Fitted with a sink and water facilities, the area, as a 'wet' space, welcomes diverse audiences for a wide range of hands-on workshops and practical activities. Next to The Lab is The Atelier, designed to host small-scale exhibitions, individual performances and multimedia works. As a particularly versatile room, The Atelier, in its very intimate and human proportions, works to create an environment that actively sparks creative talent in all its forms.

THE URBAN CORRIDOR

Geographically, the National Museum at Stamford Road forms a central axis linking Bras Basah Road and Fort Canning Park. Before the Singapore Management University (SMU) was constructed, a leafy field separated Bras Basah and the institution. In conceiving their design for the building extension, the project's architects placed much importance on the museum as an effective link between the greenery of Fort Canning Park to the south, and the city and heritage district to the north.

Though, of course, Singapore is choked with cars these days, it is with pedestrians in mind that the design team imagined the museum as a cultural destination for all in the civilised urban landscape. Indeed, for most of its long history, the Stamford Road institution has attracted crowds far bigger and broader than the city's traditionally small elite. Old photographs attest to the presence of hawkers

elling food in the museum grounds, proof of its ability to draw a wide variety of local folk. Working within the framework of the museum s an open, multi-purpose gathering place welcoming a diverse cross-section of people, national authorities have collaborated with e institution's landscape consultants, ICN Design International, to plan a wide and inviting green space fronting the façade. The old useum's boundary wall has been partially removed, direct access to the SMU campus has been established, and motor traffic from rmenian Street has been redirected north, thus freeing a broad, grassy area in front of the museum where people can meet and watch erformances in a rationally laid-out and accessible sculpture garden.

ere, those passing through as well as those entering the museum can enjoy the majestic stone sculpture of Singaporean Cultural ledallion winner Han Sai Por. Han's work is particularly well-suited to public areas because her creative interest in form goes beyond e narrow confines of the modernist 'art for art's sake' credo, the artist working her medium to dialogue with the space her sculpture ill ultimately inhabit. In the museum forecourt, a series of eight imposing striated granite monoliths called *20 Tonnes* has been ositioned zen-like in a row. The stark austerity of Han's abstract composition forms a striking contrast to the refined and classically rnamented museum façade behind, drawing visitors into the compound.

eeds, another organic and more intimate work by Han Sai Por, is sited by the banyan tree on the forecourt's east side and was ommissioned specially by the museum. The stone, carved by the artist into two forms, was excavated from the rocky base of Fort anning when the hillside was dug to build the foundations of the extension. It is quite possible that the National Museum of Singapore the only public institution in the world boasting a work of art made specifically for it, from the very rock beneath it!

index

Numbers in italics denote illustrations.

ADDITIONAL PHOTO CREDITS
The publishers would like to thank the following for permission to reproduce their photographs:
Frank Pinckers 10–11, 24–25, 26–27, 46–47
National Museum of Singapore 14 (inset), 38–39, 116 (inset)